WHAT WE
DO NOW

WHAT WE DO NOW

EDITED BY
DENNIS LOY JOHNSON
AND VALERIE MERIANS

MELVILLE HOUSE PUBLISHING
HOBOKEN, NEW JERSEY

"The Real Mandate" by Eric Foner first appeared in
The Nation magazine.

Portions of Lewis Lapham's "*Res Publica*" were adapted
from *Gag Rule* (Penguin Press, 2004).

"Reviving American Democracy" by Howard Dean first
appeared, in altered form, in *You Have the Power: Take Back
Our Country and Restore Democracy in America*, by Howard
Dean with Judith Warner (Simon & Schuster, 2004).

"Time to Get Religion" by Nicholas D. Kristof
© 2004 The New York Times Co. Reprinted with permission.

"Manifesto" by George Saunders reprinted by permission of
United Feature Syndicate, Inc.

The editors would like to thank Sophie Schiavo,
Geoff Kloske and Bernard-Henri Lévy.

Book design: David Konopka

Melville House Publishing
P.O. Box 3278
Hoboken, NJ 07030

ISBN: 0976140764

Library of Congress Cataloging-in-Publication Data on file.

TABLE OF CONTENTS

VIII INTERNATIONAL RELATIONS

IX DISSENT

APPENDIX

INTRODUCTION
MANIFESTO FOR THE POST-11/2 WORLD

There are cases which cannot be overdone by language, and this is one.
—Thomas Paine

Make no mistake: These are grim times.

On November 5, just three days after the election, Edward J. Veal, a young man of good education, who had a good white-collar job and who had recently become engaged to a young woman in Iowa, and who was described by his friends as "calm, upbeat and fun-loving," drove his car all the way from his home in Georgia to New York City, to the site where the World Trade Center once stood in lower Manhattan, climbed down into the gaping pit, and shot himself in the head with a shotgun. According to a New York Times report, friends and family said he was in despair over the election.

Other people are choosing other forms of escape: The day after the election, the Canadian government's website for immigration information received so many hundreds of thousands of hits—nearly 300,000 according to an official—that it crashed.

Suicide, leaving your country; these are desperate acts, but they bespeak the moment. People are not upset, they are distraught. Even people who are staying put, who are going through their days and trying to get over it, are not upset in the way they usually are when their candidate loses. Something is different this time. They are feeling a sense of loss, yes, but in the sense of something leaving, something beloved getting away from them. And to an unprecedented degree, people are not getting over it.

What's more, they are feeling that this grief marks their deep isolation from the other half of the country. It's hard to imagine a Republican getting so upset that they'd kill themselves, unless it's to imagine them getting so mad at the thought of Bill Clinton having consensual sex with an intern that their head explodes.

We do, indeed, seem to have become a country where moderates, let alone liberals, simply don't stand a blessed chance, where anything other than an angry, intolerant, persecutorial attitude is scorned and mocked by a plentitude of bar bullies gone drunk with power. After all, this is an election that turned on drastic issues with no middle ground: You voted for war, or you voted against it. You voted for gay people, or you voted against them. You voted for Church in government, or you voted against it. You voted for a man who stole the last election, or you voted against him.

And now we have a right-wing fundamentalist Christian government, with a leader who codified his attitude toward the rest of the world in a State of the Union address as: "You're either with us or against us."

For the 56 million people who voted against George W. Bush—more people than voted for Ronald Reagan or Bill Clinton in either of their victories, by the way—such thuggish absolutism explains why America has become a dark and ominous place. And the retrograde to a whiter, more Christian America that ignores its own "melting pot" hoo-haw seems certain to speed up: Women are certain to lose all kinds of reproductive rights, social security will be privatized, people will suffer and die in increasing numbers for lack of health care, environmental protections will be rolled back, and the president who brags about not reading will no doubt continue to flag his ignorance of civil rights issues by refusing to speak to the NAACP and insisting that it's okay to drop habeas corpus when he wants to, especially for Muslims.

Meanwhile, a bizarre atmosphere has developed whereby the media around us seems completely unaware of the problem, to a degree that seems purposeful. A year into the Iraq war, some of our major newspapers ran *mea culpas* indicating that they had just realized what the average citizen knew from the start, which was that the war was based on lies. At that point, nearly a thousand American soldiers were already dead. Yet heaven help anyone else who had made the observation in timely fashion (two words: Liberty Fries).

The media has also been profoundly out of touch with something else wracking the hearts and minds of millions of Americans: the fact that our system of democracy seems completely broken, and has seemed so since at least the 2000 election, if not the Clinton impeachment. But this is simply not open for serious discussion, let alone coverage. How many Americans are aware, for example, that a recount of the 2000 Florida vote *did* finally take place, after the Supreme Court hijacked and decided the issue, and that two separate teams of independent investigators found that Al Gore had won a state-wide count? How much coverage—serious, probing coverage—is being paid in your newspaper right now to the fact that John Kerry may have won Ohio?

Instead, the nightly news and daily newspapers have become strange places, where the critical matter that does get reported—half a million people showing up in New York to demonstrate against the president, for example—is ghettoized, while the grief and worry behind it all, the grief gripping literally millions of Americans—gripping people like Edward J. Veal—is simply unknown to privileged mainstream journalists. The deep-seated fear and anger of disenfranchised black voters in Florida—more this time than in 2000—is unknown to them. The terror of senior citizens losing health care is unknown to them. The anxiety of women losing reproductive rights is unknown to them. The ominousness of having your children forced to pray in schools to somebody else's god is unknown to them. The more than 100,000 innocent civilians killed so far in the Iraq war goes unmentioned in the overwhelming majority of mainstream media. It's not news to them.

As Tom Paine said, "These are the times that try men's souls." So much so that the feeling of hopelessness seems utterly overwhelming.

But consider: That very line from Tom Paine, which is the opening line of a dispatch he wrote while accompanying George Washington and his troops as they crossed the Delaware in retreat to Valley Forge. The dispatch, the first of thirteen pamphlets later collected as *The Crisis,* so roused the tattered bluecoats during their miserable, frozen encampment that they used that famous first line as the watchword, the password for guards and pickets, during the action that finally took them out of retreat and on to the successful surprise attack on British troops in Trenton, a major turning point in the Revolutionary War. (The pickets stopped short of demanding the second, third, and fourth marvelous lines: "The summer soldier and the sunshine patriot will, in this crisis, shrink from the service of their country; but he that stands it now, deserves the love and thanks of man and woman. Tyranny, like hell, is not easily conquered, yet we have this consolation with us, that the harder the conflict, the more glorious the triumph. What we obtain too cheap, we esteem too lightly.")

Paine, of course, made a practice of such writings. As school children used to be taught, his earlier manifesto "Common Sense" was one of the prime catalysts behind the American Revolution itself; selling over

500,000 copies in 1776, paving the way to the Declaration of Independence, and on to war. (Trevelyan: "It would be difficult to name any human composition which has had an effect at once so instant, so extended and so lasting.")

And so the thought occurred to the two editors of this volume, as we have watched, in the days since the election, a remarkable movement, millions strong, flag and stumble in grief: Let us issue a manifesto, before it is too late. Let us try to keep that energy together, and moving forward. Let us instill in people a sense that there is something they can do *right now*. Let us turn life in the post-11/2 world into a time that is, as Tom Paine said of the time at Valley Forge, "rather a ravage than a conquest." You can survive a ravaging, and live to fight again.

And so began a series of furious, 'round the clock e-mails and phone calls, as we approached as many serious thinkers and activists from as many cultural fronts as we could. We gave them only one directive: to write something about their area of expertise that fit the title of the book.

From the start, the two of us were heartened by the responses. More than one supposedly-staid intellectual whooped down the phone line when they heard from us. Not one asked about payment. People with hellacious schedules beyond imagining dropped everything to stay up all night and get down their thoughts. Others, fearful of their ability to articulate their ideas before the short deadline, probed their published works for something appropriate to retool, so eager were they to take part. Within seven days, we had a manuscript.

It is not without holes. There are many issues we wanted to cover that we simply could not for various reasons of time constraint. There are disagreements in these pages, too. Yet it is, on the whole, a remarkable cauldron of ideas, and a moving enunciation of the still-throbbing resistance to the rise of the fundamentalist right. Most importantly, it outlines reasons to hope, and things to do—*now.*

It confirms, in other words, another story you might have missed in the news, although it is under wide discussion on the Internet and other emerging news sources. It is a debunking of the pernicious notion that

America is divided cleanly between Red and Blue states. This, of course, is true only in the sense of the Electoral College, with its bullying winner-take-all basis. But use the same color code to represent the country in a map of the popular vote—after all, the thing that seems closest to "democracy" to most people—and you find that this is actually a country gone purple.

With rage? Let us hope not, although no one should deny that anger is a component of our grief. But let us use that as a simple motivator, and let the notion that we can do something now assuage the grief and dispel the panic. As Tom Paine wrote in the manifesto that inspired this one: "Panics, in some cases, have their uses; they produce as much good as hurt. Their duration is always short; the mind soon grows through them, and acquires a firmer habit than before. But their peculiar advantage is, that they are the touchstones of sincerity and hypocrisy, and bring things and men to light, which might otherwise have lain forever undiscovered."

Lose your grief, find your courage, and fight for your country.

Dennis Loy Johnson
2 December 2004

ATTITUDE

RES PUBLICA
LEWIS LAPHAM

Rightly understood, democracy is an uproar, and if we mean to engage the argument about the course of the American future, let us hope that it proves to be loud, disorderly, bitter, and fierce.

Lewis Lapham is the editor of *Harper's Magazine*, and the author of numerous books, including *Theater of War, Hotel America, Money and Class in America, 30 Satires,* and, most recently, *Gag Rule.* He has hosted two television series for PBS, *America's Century* and *Bookmark,* and his writing has appeared in *Vanity Fair, The New York Times, The Wall Street Journal, The London Observer, The National Review, Fortune, Forbes,* and elsewhere.

Twenty-five years ago in the American political vocabulary, the word "public" carried with it the connotation of a striving toward the common good—public health, public interest, public servant, public school. The word "private" referred to the personal and selfish interest—private trout stream, private tax exemption, private plane. The gaudy accumulations of wealth said to have sprung full-blown from the head of President Ronald Reagan reconfigured the sense and usage of the words. "Public" now serves as a synonym for incompetence, futility, and fraud; "private" implies excellence, efficiency, and noble purpose, and for at least two generations the Democratic Party has declined to quarrel with the notions that sustain the Republican dream of heaven:

That the best government is no government.

That global capitalism is the eighth wonder of the world, a light unto the nations and the answer to everybody's prayers.

That nothing must interfere with the benign and omniscient judgment of the free market.

That the art of politics, embarrassingly human and therefore corrupt, is subordinate to the science of economics, reassuringly abstract and therefore perfect.

That the well-ordered state is synonymous with the well-managed retail outlet, democracy a fancy Greek name for the American Express card and the Neiman Marcus Christmas catalogue.

That history is at an end. Having reached a final stopping place on the road to ideological perfection, mankind no longer needs trouble itself with any new political ideas.

As a consequence of the Democratic Party's failure to produce an antithetical set of propositions, much less to trouble itself with new political ideas, we've let fall into disrepair nearly all of the public infrastructure—roads, water systems, schools, power plants, bridges, hospitals, broadcast frequencies—that provides the country with the foundation of its common enterprise. The lopsided division of the country into the factions of the deprived many and the privileged few has downgraded our faith in discounting what the brokers classify as "non-market values," we're left an American *res publica* defined not as a union of its collective energies and hopes but as an aggregate of loosely affiliated selfish interests (ethnic, regional, commercial, sexual) armed with their own manifestos, loyal to their own agendas, secure in the gated communities of their own fear.

The laissez-faire theories of government do us an injustice. They don't speak to the best of our character, neither do they express the cherished ideal embodied in the history of a courageous people. What joins Americans one to another is not a common nationality, race or ancestry, but their voluntary pledge to a shared work of both the moral and political imagination. The love of country follows from the love of its freedoms, not from a pride in its armies or its fleets. Understood as useful and well-made instruments meant to support the liberties of the people (tools on the order of a plow, an ax, or a surveyor's plumb line), the institutions of democratic government provide the premise for a narrative rather than the design for a monument or the plans for an invasion.

The barbarism in Washington doesn't dress itself in the costumes of Al Qaeda; it wears instead the smooth-shaven smile of a Senate resolution sold to the highest bidder, and if we are to account for, and possibly correct, the country's reversals of fortune over the last four years, we might begin by remembering that politics are the means with which we make our freedom. The shaping of a decent American future presupposes an argument between time past and time present, between the inertia implicit in the weight of things-as-they-are and the energy inherent in the hope of things-as-they-might-become. The supporters of the status quo invariably command the popular majority; theirs is the party of the Disney Company and the Bush administration, putting out more flags, enlarging the radius of the secure perimeter, distributing the pillows of cant.

Only by finding its way out of the Republican Garden of Eden can the Democratic Party rediscover itself as the party of things-as-they-might-become, acknowledging the truth of Alfred North Whitehead's observation that it is the business of the future to be dangerous—not because the future is perverse but because it doesn't know how to be anything else. Democracy allies itself with change and proceeds from the assumption that nobody knows enough, that nothing is final, that the old order (whether of men or institutions) will be dragged offstage when its prescriptions no longer fit the facts. The freedoms of expression present democratic societies with the unwelcome news that they are in trouble, but because all societies, like most individuals, are always in some kind of trouble, the news doesn't drive them onto the reefs of destruction. They die instead from the fear of thought and the paralysis that accompanies the wish to believe that only the wicked perish.

Whether we like it or not, the argument now going forward in the United States is the same argument that put an end to the Roman and Weimar Republics, built the scaffolds of the Spanish Inquisition, gave rise to the American Revolution. If we fail to engage it, we do so at our peril. It is not the law that takes freedom from us but the laziness of our own minds. Dostoyevsky put the proposition in the voice of the Grand Inquisitor, who understood that the power of the Catholic Church rested on the reliably human wish to remain a slave, to prefer the comforts of magic, mystery, and authority, whenever possible to check into the nearest cage. Nobody ever said that democratic government was easy, which is why, during the twenty years between the last century's two world wars, it failed and was abandoned by the people of Italy, Turkey, Portugal, Spain, Bulgaria, Greece, Romania, Yugoslavia, Hungary, Albania, Poland, Estonia, Latvia, Lithuania, Austria, and Germany.

Jefferson believed that the tree of liberty needed to be nourished every now and then with the blood of revolution. I don't know whether the time has come again to storm the palace and seize the radio station, but the government now in Washington doesn't meet the specifications of the one envisioned in the Declaration of Independence. The signers of the Declaration staked their lives, their fortunes, and their sacred honor on the proposition that when government becomes oppressively corrupt, it is not only the right but also the duty of the people to revolt. So it was said and believed in Philadelphia in 1776; so it can be said and believed nearly anywhere in the United States in 2004. We have a government in Washington that doesn't defend the liberty of the American people, steals from the poor to feed the rich, finds its wealth and happiness in the waging of ceaseless war. Where else do we turn except to politics, and how else do our politics get made if not with the voices of dissent?

Rightly understood, democracy is an uproar, and if we mean to engage the argument about the course of the American future, let us hope that it proves to be loud, disorderly, bitter, and fierce.

Every society can always count on the parties of reaction crying up the wish to make time stand still, seeking to hide from the storm of the world behind the walls of monumental bureaucracy or within the choruses of adoring praise. Democratic self-government proceeds from a more courageous principle, allying itself with the proposition that the future is no farther away and no more alarming than the next best guess, the next play from scrimmage, the next sentence. At college in the 1950s I was taught to think of the twentieth century as the miraculous and happy ending to the story of human progress; I now think of the twenty-first century as a still-primitive beginning. From the perspective of the thirtieth century I expect the historians to look back on the works of our modern world as if on sand castles built by careless but sometimes surprisingly gifted children. Idealism rescues cynicism, and the presence of many individuals free to try the strength of their own imagination and intelligence assumes a ceaseless making and remaking, of laws and customs as well as of fortunes and matinee idols.

Among all the country's political virtues, candor is the one most necessary to the health and well-being of our mutual enterprise. Unless we try to tell one another the truth about what we know and think and see, we might as well amuse ourselves—for as long as somebody in uniform allows us to do so—with fairy tales. To the extent that a democratic society gives its citizens the chance to speak in their own voices and listens to what they have to say, it gives itself the chance not only of discovering its multiple glories and triumphs but also of surviving its multiple follies and crimes.

THE REAL MANDATE
ERIC FONER

The left must do what it has always done in American history—what Frederick Douglass and Susan B. Anthony and Eugene Debs did: stake out a clear position in favor of social and economic justice, at home and abroad, and articulate it as clearly and forcefully as possible.

Eric Foner is DeWitt Clinton Professor of History at Columbia University. His most recent book is the survey textbook of American history, *Give Me Liberty!*

Rarely has a presidential election produced such widespread despair on the left. By any objective standard, George W. Bush has been among the worst presidents in American history. One of the main purposes of elections in a democracy is to act as a check on those in power by confronting them with the possibility of being removed from office. If Bush can be reelected after having alienated virtually the entire world, brought the country into war on false pretenses, and mortgaged the nation's future to provide economic benefits to the rich, what incentive will other presidents have to act more reasonably?

Nonetheless, the vote was not a mandate for a conservative agenda. A majority of fifty-one percent and a margin of three percent in the popular vote do not constitute a landslide, no matter what Karl Rove and the spin doctors insist. Indeed, the most striking thing about the result is how it resembled that of 2000. All but three states voted the same way they did the last time around. The nation remains closely divided.

Progressives must not succumb to hopelessness. The left must do what it has always done in American history—what Frederick Douglass and Susan B. Anthony and Eugene Debs did: stake out a clear position in favor of social and economic justice, at home and abroad, and articulate it as clearly and forcefully as possible. We must also work to strengthen institutions that provide the social basis for progressive politics. The right has its evangelical churches, often the only remaining centers of civil society in a de-centered world of shopping malls and galloping subdivisions. The left traditionally had unions, and their decline is intimately related to Democratic defeat. Even without strong unions, Kerry did best among voters with lower incomes. Nothing would revive progressive politics more effectively than a reinvigoration of American unions. This may not be the road to immediate electoral success. But when Democrats return to power, as they surely will one day, it is essential that there be a progressive agenda in place to help shape public policies.

We must not join the bandwagon proclaiming that "moral values" were the key to this election. In exit polls, the "moral values" category was a grab-bag indicating everything from hostility to abortion rights to the desire for a leader who says what he means and apparently means what he says. Denigrating religious conviction per se is hardly the path to follow. But progressives must not seek victory by appealing to intolerance and unreason and rejecting the traditions of the Enlightenment that we alone seem to embrace today. We should take comfort from the fact that our values—social justice, respect for international law, religious and moral toleration—are shared by the rest of the industrialized world. One of these days, the United States will catch up.

I suspect that the attacks of September 11 and the sense of being engaged in a worldwide war on terror contributed substantially to Bush's victory. Generally speaking, Americans have not changed presidents in the midst of a war. The Bush campaign consistently and successfully appealed to fear, with continuous warnings of imminent and future attacks. Land of the free? Perhaps. Home of the brave? Not any more.

LIGHT UP THE CAVE
ALICIA OSTRIKER

We have to say whatever nobody else will.

Twice nominated for a National Book Award, Alicia Ostriker is the author of nine volumes of poetry, including *The Crack in Everything* and *The Little Space: Poems Selected and New, 1968-1998*. She teaches at Rutgers University.

"It is in not incumbent on you to finish the task. Neither are you free to give it up."

— *The Ethics of the Fathers*

So the election is over, and we lost. After two and a half years of demonstrating against the war, writing and signing petitions, writing and sending poems to each other, sending money to MoveOn, and its many brother and sister organizations, registering strangers on the phone, getting on buses to electioneer in Pennsylvania, knocking on doors, handing out literature, handing out poems to people in the streets, slapping bumper stickers on our cars and Kerry pins on our lapels, we lost.

My favorite pin was one that said "Liberty and Justice for Oil." It made my students, or at least some of them, smile. I told them that they could turn me in to the thought police if they wanted to. Didn't they think that we already had more liberty and justice than we actually needed, and that it made sense to trade some of it in—via the Patriot Act— for oil? Another pin, this one truly wicked, used a photo taken during the President's audience with the Pope. The Pope is sitting in his white dress and skullcap with his head in his hands, while the President sits in a chair nearby wearing the same slightly perplexed face we saw in the Michael Moore film. The caption says, "It said Abomination, so I bombed a nation." My students are learning, I trust, the uses of irony.

Without humor, we are done for. Of course, some things are not funny. One October evening, returning from a day canvassing in Pennsylvania, a tall, handsome 50-ish WASP man across the aisle from me on the bus recounted the conversation he had with one woman after asking her if she had decided whom she was voting for and what her issues were.

She: We're voting for George W. Bush. We're Christian people and he's a good Christian man.

He: Okay. Is there anything you might disagree with him about, or feel he could have done differently?

She: Yes. On 9/12 he should have just gone in there and demolished Iraq.

He (after a pause): But you know that the suicide bombers on 9/11 weren't Iraqis. Most of them were Saudis.

She: It makes no difference. They're all the same.

So we lost, partly because the Bush campaign—aided by a supine press and media establishment—successfully played on the fear and ignorance of people like this woman. But do I think Christians, or Midwesterners, or Southerners, are all the same? No way. I look at the sweep of red on the map, and feel as if my bit of blue is being pushed into the sea. Then I remember that the glass is 48% full. The land I love is inhabited by citizens *in every state* who deplore pre-emptive war, who think stealing from the poor to give to the rich is not a moral value, who believe women's and men's bodies are their own, and who cherish the natural environment. It is a beginning. It is not the end. I think the grassroots activism we have seen, the amazingly exuberant, smart, organized young people who fuel it, and the web that is its tool, will not go away.

I have never been much of an organization person. This is the first campaign I ever worked in. What made campaigning thrilling for me was the exuberance and competence of the young organizers. Tall, gorgeous Samantha, who gave up a well-paying job as a law clerk to volunteer for the League of Conservation Voters. Jesse, who taught us what to say when we were phone banking. Julie, who trained us in the arts of eye contact when canvassing, with a baby in her arms. The army of young people who prepared the flyers, the bagels, the coffee. The creators of an anti-war poetry reading at St. Mark's Church in the East Village that drew thousands of us to weep and cheer.

The day after the election, the sophomores in my Introduction to Poetry class want me to give them websites to go to for information. A few weeks ago we read Yeats' great poem "The Second Coming," with its famous lines about the blood-dimmed tide being loosed on the world, and the concise political summary, "The best lack all conviction, while the worst/ Are full of passionate intensity." Some of them have just voted for the first time and are furious. They are worried, with reason, about the draft and about Roe v. Wade. One young woman raises her hand to say that she thinks democracy is like a Weeble. A what? Weebles, she explains, are those big bottom-heavy dolls that you can push over, and they wobble but then they come back.

Perhaps she is right. Probably the state of the nation will get worse before it gets better. But now we can hear each other, we can talk, we can plan. I like the Martin Luther King quote that says, "The arc of history is long, but it bends toward justice." As a poet, I feel the tug of that arc pulling me forward; I know other poets feel the same.

"In a time of universal deceit, telling the truth is a revolutionary act," as George Orwell reminds us in his essay "Politics and the English Language." We poets represent an infinite world of truths that cannot be told except in the form of poetry.

So we have our job cut out for us, since universal deceit is growing like a bamboo forest around us. We have to include the fact of the vitality of lies, the vigor and power of deceit in our pictures of the world—even or especially when we turn inward. We have to say whatever nobody else will. "Art destroys silence," Dmitri Shostakovich wrote in tribute to Yevtushenko's poem "Babi Yar," a poem of extraordinary courage on the topic of Russian complicity in the Holocaust. And we need to remember not only satire, not only anger and fear but how and what to love. Some of us will be quoting Adam Zagajewski's "Try to Praise the Mutilated World":

Try to praise the mutilated world.

Remember June's long days,
and wild strawberries, drops of wine, the dew.

The nettles that methodically overgrow
the abandoned homesteads of exiles.

You must praise the mutilated world.

You watched the stylish yachts and ships;
one of them had a long trip ahead of it,
while salty oblivion awaited others.

You've seen the refugees heading nowhere,
you've heard the executioners sing joyfully.

You should praise the mutilated world.

Remember the moments when we were together
in a white room and the curtain fluttered.

Return in thought to the concert where music flared.

You gathered acorns in the park in autumn
and leaves eddied over the earth's scars.

Praise the mutilated world
and the grey feather a thrush lost,
and the gentle light that strays and vanishes
and returns.

Or we might be quoting the Nobel laureate Wislawa Szymborska's
wonderfully anti-utopian poem "Possibilities:"

I prefer movies.
I prefer cats.
I prefer the oaks along the Warta.
I prefer Dickens to Dostoyevsky.
I prefer myself liking people
to myself loving mankind.
I prefer keeping a needle and thread on hand, just in case.
I prefer the color green.
I prefer not to maintain

that reason is to blame for everything.
I prefer exceptions.
I prefer to leave early.
I prefer talking to doctors about something else.
I prefer the old fine-lined illustrations.
I prefer the absurdity of writing poems
to the absurdity of not writing poems.
I prefer, where love's concerned, nonspecific anniversaries
that can be celebrated every day.
I prefer moralists
who promise me nothing.
I prefer cunning kindness to the over-trustful kind.
I prefer the earth in civvies.
I prefer conquered to conquering countries.
I prefer having some reservations.
I prefer the hell of chaos to the hell of order.
I prefer Grimms' fairy tales to the newspapers' front pages.
I prefer leaves without flowers to flowers without leaves.
I prefer dogs with uncropped tails.
I prefer light eyes, since mine are dark.
I prefer desk drawers.
I prefer many things that I haven't mentioned here
to many things I've also left unsaid.
I prefer zeroes on the loose
to those lined up behind a cipher.
I prefer the time of insects to the time of stars.
I prefer to knock on wood.
I prefer not to ask how much longer and when.
I prefer keeping in mind even the possibility
that existence has its own reason for being.

East European poets are experts at how to live with irony under the
shadow of tyranny, lighting a candle *and* cursing the darkness. I will be
reading more of them. I will be reading more of Allen Ginsberg,

Muriel Rukeyser, Adrienne Rich, Carolyn Forché, Sharon Doubiago, William Carlos Williams, C.K. Williams, Gerald Stern, Lucille Clifton, H.D., Denise Levertov, Maxine Kumin, Langston Hughes, Gary Snyder, Denise Levertov—our own homegrown visionaries, poets who know how to love and how to hope. "In a dark time, the eye begins to see," says Theodore Roethke. I'll be listening to old Woody Guthrie and early Bob Dylan. Yes, it's true, it's a hard, it's a hard, it's a hard, it's a hard, it's a hard rain gonna fall. For the immediate present, I will remind myself of some lines by the poet Anne Sexton:

> Depression is boring, I think,
> And I would do better to make
> Some soup and light up the cave.

RED STATES?
PERCIVAL EVERETT

*We need to actually be liberal, to view the world as being made up of varying
points of view and to court those we would not normally meet for coffee.*

Percival Everett is the author of several books, including *Erasure, Glyph, Frenzy, Watershed,* and *Damned If I Do: Stories.* He is a professor of English at the University of Southern California and lives in Los Angeles.

It's easy for us to become despondent in the face of recent events. We have watched as obvious and glaring lies have been sold to a large portion of the American public. We are watching still as a so-called war against terrorism rages in the wrong place, killing countless innocent people while our people count "insurgents" who are behaving just as we would if we had been invaded. We, for the most part, would resist proudly. But somehow, despite the patriotism, the nationalism, the jingoism, and our knowledge of names on the roster of lost American lives, it all remains somehow unreal to us and safe. The poor families of the dead soldiers of course do not want their children to have died in vain and so they adopt the party line that this is a justified war. Fox and CNN have managed to clean up carnage in a way that separates grieving parents from other grieving parents. It is much better that my son be a hero than a fool. But this is not what scares me most.

The networks, all of them, failed at every turn to be direct with the American people. I refer now to the televised debates between Kerry and Bush. It took no genius to see the difference in intellectual capacity between the two men. Bush, in the first debate, said that the insurgents were resisting "vociferously". This from a man never known for understatement and especially not known for his use of irony. Bush came across as an idiot and what we were left with was an army of so-called intelligent heads making comments like, "He was better than any of us expected" and "Kerry certainly didn't score a knockout." Bush's repetition of his key phrases, his constant repetition, his alarming repetition, his annoying repetition, his annoying repetition... well, you get the point. If the repetition bothers us here, then why not during the debates. It is sad to think that just over half of the voters like Bush because he is like their stupid neighbor, an any man, an anyone, as in "Anyone can grow up to be president."

Many of us are disappointed. That is the way it goes. Nearly half the country was going to be disappointed regardless of the outcome of the election. I can deal with the disappointment of my candidate having lost. I cannot deal with the lies. But we lost because of lies. We lost to slogans. And here is the difference between liberals and conservatives these days.

The conservatives have sold to the public a couple of lies that have taken hold and with them come a sensibility that is hard to undo. The lies are that there is a "liberal" media and that there is a thing called "political correctness". Here, I will not even venture into a discussion of these lies, but offer that we liberals have been unable to undo them because 1) the lies have given rise to a distrust of intellectuals and liberal thinkers and 2) because we liberals cannot answer a goddamn question in less than eight fucking pages. We're too busy thinking about what is true and reasonable to realize we're being robbed. We walk around the holly bush to step in the gopher hole. We find slogans distasteful, I more than anyone probably, but we had better find a couple.

The race for the White House in 2008 has already started. And the advantage goes to the liars. It goes to them because they have managed to divide the country into red and blue states. They have sucked us into blaming the loss of the election on the backward red states in the middle of the country. We sit around laughing about the yokels without waterfront and all the while we alienate the people who are just like us. Kerry lost by few votes in the red states and won by few in the blue. If people in the so-called red states can be led to believe that they belong to the heartland of RED STATES, then another avenue of reasonable discourse has been clogged by our inability to accept all kinds of people. We need to actually be liberal, to view the world as being made up of varying points of view and to court those we would not normally meet for coffee. We had better give up that Us/Them mentality. You know, the one we find so disgusting when employed by lesser thinkers, the mentality of Bush when it comes to dealing with the rest of the world.

Forgive my speedy coverage here. I will add that there is one more diabolical element in place for control of future elections. It is the "No Child Left Behind" program of the Bush administration. The logic is impeccable. No child will be left behind, because no children are going anywhere. It is a failure and will be and will serve to create a population of capable, but naïve and slow Americans who will respond to slogans and repetition and ads, ads, ads. We have a lot of educating to do, of ourselves and of our neighbors and we need to all know that getting smarter, being well educated, wanting to explore problems, wanting to be challenged are good things. I honestly do not believe that more than half this country is dumber than George Bush. I won't accept it. I will accept as true that smart, honest people are often the victims of con artists.

PLANS OF ATTACK

PUNCHING THE BULLY: A FIVE-STEP PLAN
STEVE ALMOND

Liberal special interests need to build a coalition powerful enough to convince liberal politicians to come out of hiding. These politicians need to provide some concrete sense of what the left would do with power, in contrast to the right.

Steve Almond is the author of *My Life in Heavy Metal* and *Candyfreak: A Journey Through the Chocolate Underbelly of America*. His new collection, *The Evil B.B. Chow and Other Stories*, is forthcoming in spring, 2005.

Step One: Grow Some Balls

Stop drifting toward the center, in the errant hope that the American people will view us as a kinder, gentler Republican Party.

We need to reconnect with the core principles of the Left—that which differentiates us from the right—and assert these with some moral urgency.

These principles (just as a reminder) include:

Government should be a force for good in the lives of the disenfranchised.

America is a secular state founded on freedom of, *and from*, religion.

Poverty is morally wrong, as are obscene concentrations of wealth.

The interests of people should come before the interests of corporations.

The vast majority of our citizens agree with these ideas. Yet the conservative movement has been able to seize all three branches of government while flouting every single one of them.

This began long before George W. Bush, or his secret weapon Osama Bin Laden, came along. The political right has been working for 30 years to rebuild their party by appealing to the worst impulses of our citizenry: fear, sloth, grievance, greed, and denial.

The basic posture of the Left, meanwhile, has been one of moral accommodation. Rather than confronting the basic cruelties of conservatism, we have allowed deceitful, hate-mongering politicians to bully us.

But you don't accommodate bullies. You don't play nice and hope they'll stop. You punch them in the mouth. Period.

You make them pay a price for lying to the American people. You attack using the most obvious weapon: truth.

Step Two: Applied Learning

1. When a right wing politician decides, as Bush did, for political reasons, to seize on a moral issue such as gay marriage, the proper response is not to compete for evangelical brownie points. It's to point out that *they are being bigots.*

Two gay people getting married has nothing to do with marriage as an institution. It has to do with homophobes who are so insecure about their own marriages (or sexuality) that they have to obsess over others.

2. When a politician proposes huge tax cuts for the affluent, the proper response is to point out that he is fostering inequality and greed.

It is to call him a liar—directly, that word, *liar*—every time he tries to sell his tax plan as "tax relief for the middle class." Then to provide a concrete example: the top one percent of Americans received a $60,000 tax cut.

3. When politicians redraw congressional district lines expressly to distort the will of the electorate, the proper response is to accuse them of treason.

4. When a president proposes to go to war against another nation not as an act of self-defense, but as a matter of ideological discretion, you call for his impeachment.

You do this *before* his intelligence proves spurious, *before* the body count begins, *before* the war turns into a quagmire. You do this because it is morally wrong to launch a war against a nation that does not pose a threat to Americans.

5. When the president allows industry lobbyists to write policy, then gives his initiatives names like "The Healthy Forest Initiative" you are morally compelled to paint him as corrupt, and an enemy of nature.

I could go on and on and on, but the basic dynamic is the same: when faced with a bully, you don't convene focus groups, or consult polling data, or pundits. You speak the truth, as bluntly as possible.

Step Three: Stop Nominating Stiffs
Apparently, suffering Mondale, Dukakis, and Gore wasn't quite enough.

I don't want to get bogged down enumerating all of Kerry's mistakes, but the major ones bear citation.

The 2004 Democratic Convention marked the apotheosis of Lefty Wimp. Faced with an incumbent whose record was, at best, disastrous, the Dems threw a militarized pep rally. Rather than establish lines of attack against Bush, they attempted to paint themselves as the *nice guys with guns.* This framed the election in precisely the terms the right desired: as a battle for national security in a time of war.

Amazingly, Kerry failed to apprehend the basic emotional and psychological shape of the race.

That is: rather than defend his record, Bush was merely going to attack Kerry as an effete, Massachusetts liberal, and portray himself as steadfast everyman. It was this perception that Kerry needed to destroy.

He had plenty of opportunities.

On the day the Swift Boat Veterans began running their ads, John Kerry should have called a press conference and said the following:

"I believe, in this time of war, that the American people deserve a full accounting of the choices we made during the war of our youth. Therefore, I challenge George W. Bush to stand beside me and to answer questions, once and for all, about his service. I will do the same. The President has ordered tens of thousands of young men and women into battle. The very least he can do is explain why *he* sought to avoid combat, and why, even more astonishingly, records indicate that he was AWOL. A President as resolute as Mr. Bush should embrace the chance to clarify his record. He would be a coward if he did not. Worse still, he would leave the impression that he has something to hide."

He should have issued this challenge every single day. Instead, he sat around whining to his advisors.

The central unchallenged fallacy of the election was this "Bush is strong" nonsense. Kerry needed to assert that his opponent was, and is, fundamentally weak, and that his refusal to admit to mistakes, or withstand doubt, is a testament to his weakness.

Kerry's best chance to unmask Bush was during the debates.

Again, I won't labor his mistakes. I will only suggest that he could have won the election rather handily had he said the following, directly to Bush's face:

"You can dress up in a fighter pilot costume and pray with families after you've sent their sons and daughters to die, but you can't know war. Because everyone in this auditorium knows, Mr. President, that back when you had a chance to defend American values overseas, you used your father's connections to avoid combat. I've been shot at, sir. And you can be sure I'm not going to send the sons and daughters of America into a barrage of bullets based on false information and the whim of a coward."

It was up to Kerry, in other words, to determine the moral discourse of the race. It was up to him to draw his own portrait of the president, judging him by his actions, not his rhetoric. He failed miserably.

Step Four: Wake Up and Smell the Newsprint: The Media Is No Longer Interested in the Truth

One of the most fascinating documents to emerge from the 2004 election was *Newsweek*'s in-depth, insider saga.

The piece documented, in numbing detail, the dithering of the Kerry crew, and the astonishing hubris of the Bushies.

What made it so revealing, though, was this simple fact: of the 10,000-plus carefully crafted words, not a single one made reference to the effects of either man's proposed policies on the 250 million citizens he sought to govern.

Instead, the campaign was rendered as an elaborate popularity narrative only obscurely related to the public good. In the end, the election was not viewed as a political event, but as a reality TV drama.

The media no longer discuss policy. They no longer view themselves as guardians. This is why Bush's environmental record, and his dazzling fiscal irresponsibility, for instance, never became prominent issues.

Today's reporters are merely on hand to froth telegenicslly and to track the ebb and flow of perceived power: scandal, polls, fundraising.

The basic rule in campaign coverage runs likes so: the meanest (or most embarrassing) thing said each day is tomorrow's lead. Period.

This is why Lynne Cheney—the wife of the vice-president, for God's sake—managed to grab the lead story back in June, by criticizing John Kerry for using the word "sensitive" in reference to combating terrorism.

The left needs to recognize this new paradigm. The media is no longer in the business of truth, or advocacy of the public good. They are in the business of clamor. They use the myth of objectivity as a perpetual excuse for failing to discern the truth.

There is a reason, in other words, that John Stewart (a comedian) has become our most forceful media watchdog. Because he is one of the only people who will speak about the absurdity of our coverage from within the bubble.

The left would do well to follow his example.

Kerry should have excoriated the media for replaying the Swift Boat ads while failing to report on the merits of the accusations themselves. He should have shamed them by invoking that arcane concept known as journalistic integrity.

More broadly, the left needs to borrow a page from the conservative movement: pound your message home by accusing the media of bias.

In the end, the right is best served by a media that is slavishly devoted to shallow coverage. This is why Clinton was nearly impeached based on a personal indiscretion. It is why Bush was allowed to take office without a full count of Florida's votes.

The left is best served by a media that exposes the effects of policy. They need to attack any source of media that fails to do so, that indulges in boosterism, or the politics of personal destruction.

Step Five: Start Mobilizing the Base *Now*
As despicable as their policies may be, Bush and his people know how to mobilize citizens. They do so by consciously appealing to the base.

Witness his first action as president: he cut off funding to any international family planning agencies that promoted safe sex. This was a direct sop to the religious right.

What Bush—or more accurately, Karl Rove—decided early on was that turning out 95 percent of the base works better than winning 60 percent of the undecideds.

The power of the right comes from two factions: the true believers (pro-life activists, evangelicals, gun owners) and the super-rich who actually benefit from Bush's regressive economic policies and fund the party.

Let's add to this a third faction, the angry white media, who serve as a de facto mouthpiece for conservative policy.

Despite the fact that conservatives, in large part, run this country, they remain aggrieved. This sense of grievance is what fuels them, in the same way idealism used to fuel the left.

I'm not suggesting that the Left should adopt this fundamentally bogus posture. But they do need to adopt some of the Right's more effective practices.

This means that liberal special interests (the pro-choice movement, gays, the greens, the peace movement) need to build a coalition powerful enough to convince liberal politicians to come out of hiding. These politicians need to propose specific measures that will provide some concrete sense of what the left would do with power, in contrast to the right.

They need to reassert the environment and reproductive choice and poverty as national issues, rather than kowtowing to the scare tactics. Stop trafficking in the language and tropes of the right.

Look: on the day after Bush was installed as president, Karl Rove was crunching voting data and setting goals for voter registration. Back in March, the Bush campaign had volunteers in every single precinct in Ohio. Kerry had a staff of twelve.

This is what we're up against. And it's going to require a fundamental retrenching to take the country back.

It's no longer enough for lefties to find religion at the eleventh hour. They need to start planning for 2006 and 2008, right now. We live in an age of perpetual grievance and frantic inattention. This country has fallen away from Christian charity, tolerance, and forgiveness.

The left, in other words, needs a clear sense of mission. More than aiming to win some elections, they need to create a new, more humane discourse.

This is the precise historical moment that America should be leading the world in a moral sense. We, above all nations, must find a way to summon the better angels of our nature.

TIME TO GET RELIGION
NICHOLAS D. KRISTOF

I wish that winning were just a matter of presentation. But it's not. It involves compromising on principles.

Nicholas Kristof is a Pulitzer Prize-winning columnist for *The New York Times*. He grew up in Oregon, attended Harvard and Oxford, and has reported from six continents for *The Times*.

If Democrats want to know how to win again, they have a model. It's the British Labor Party.

When I studied in England in the early 1980's, the British Labor Party seemed as quaint and eccentric as Oxford itself, where we wore gowns for exams and some dons addressed the rare female student as "sir." Labor was caught in its own echo chamber of militant unions and anti-American activists, and it so repulsed voters that it seemed it might wither away entirely.

Then Tony Blair and another M.P., Gordon Brown, dragged the party away from socialism, unions, nuclear disarmament and anti-Americanism. Together they created "New Labor," which aimed for the center and aggressively courted Middle Britain instead of trying to scare it. The result is that since 1997, Mr. Blair and Labor have utterly dominated Britain.

The Democrats need a similar rebranding. But the risk is that the party will blame others for its failures—or, worse, blame the American people for their stupidity (as London's *Daily Mirror* screamed in a Page 1 headline this week: "How can 59,054,087 people be so DUMB?").

As moderates from the heartland, like Tom Daschle, are picked off by the Republicans, the party's image risks being defined even more by bicoastal, tree-hugging, gun-banning, French-speaking, Bordeaux-sipping, *Times*-toting liberals, whose solution is to veer left and galvanize the base. But firing up the base means turning off swing voters. Gov. Mike Johanns, a Nebraska Republican, told me that each time Michael Moore spoke up for John Kerry, Mr. Kerry's support in Nebraska took a dive.

Mobilizing the base would mean nominating Hillary Rodham Clinton in 2008 and losing yet again. (Mrs. Clinton has actually undertaken just the kind of makeover that I'm talking about: in the Senate, she's been cooperative, mellow and moderate, winning over upstate New Yorkers. She could do the same in the heartland if she had 50 years.)

So Democrats need to give a more prominent voice to Middle American, wheat-hugging, gun-shooting, Spanish-speaking, beer-guzzling, Bible-toting centrists. (They can tote *The Times*, too, in a plain brown wrapper.) For a nominee who could lead the Democrats to victory, think of John Edwards, Bill Richardson or Evan Bayh, or anyone who knows the difference between straw and hay.

I wish that winning were just a matter of presentation. But it's not. It involves compromising on principles. Bill Clinton won his credibility in the heartland partly by going home to Little Rock during the 1992 campaign to preside over the execution of a mentally disabled convict named Ricky Ray Rector.

There was a moral ambiguity about Mr. Clinton's clambering to power over Mr. Rector's corpse. But unless Democrats compromise, they'll be proud and true and losers.

So what do the Democrats need to do? Here are four suggestions:

Don't be afraid of religion. Offer government support for faith-based programs to aid the homeless, prisoners and AIDS victims. And argue theology with Republicans: there's much more biblical ammunition to support liberals than conservatives.

Pick battles of substance, not symbolism. The battle over Georgia's Confederate flag cost Roy Barnes his governorship and perhaps Max Cleland his Senate seat, but didn't help one working mother or jobless worker. It was a gift to Republicans.

Accept that today, gun control is a nonstarter. Instead of trying to curb guns, try to reduce gun deaths through better rules on licensing and storage, and on safety devices like trigger locks.

Hold your nose and work with President Bush as much as you can because it's lethal to be portrayed as obstructionists. Sure, block another Clarence Thomas, but here's a rule of thumb: if an otherwise qualified Supreme Court nominee would turn the clock back 10 years, approve; back 25 years, vote no; back a half-century, filibuster.

"The first thing we have to do is shake the image of us as the obstructionist party," notes Senator Ben Nelson of Nebraska, who manages to thrive as a Democrat in the red sea. He says Democrats must show a willingness to compromise, to get things done, to defer to local sensibilities. "We have to show the American people," he says, "that Democrats aren't going to take away your guns, aren't going to take away your flags."

Rethinking the Democratic Party will be wrenching. But just ask Tony Blair—it's not as wrenching as sliding into irrelevance.

FOUR PRINCIPLES FOR FOUR YEARS:
A VERY SHORT SURVIVAL MANUAL
CASS R. SUNSTEIN

This right-wing agenda for constitutional reform must be exposed and countered.

Cass R. Sunstein is the Karl N. Llewellyn Distinguished Service Professor of Jurisprudence at the University of Chicago, Law School and Department of Political Science. He is author, most recently, of *Republic.com*, *The Second Bill of Rights* and *Why Societies Need Dissent*.

Those who didn't vote for President Bush can do well for themselves, and for their country, if they follow four simple principles. Of these, the most crucial—the prerequisite for the rest—is probably the last. But first things first.

Whenever President Bush has a good idea, work with him. No party has a monopoly on good ideas. Some of President Bush's proposals have a lot of promise; let's help him with them. Consider some examples:

President Bush is right to argue for litigation reform. Too much of the time, juries come up with unpredictable and excessive damage awards, in a way that can really hurt doctors, patients, and ordinary consumers. A sensible legal system does not ask twelve random people to assign dollar values to pain and suffering, or to generate, from thin air, a specific amount to punish misconduct. The national government can and should act to make the system more rational.

In the environmental area, President Bush was battered by the Democrats for his Clear Skies Initiative, but there are some excellent ideas there. The President's innovative proposal provided a good start to producing significant reductions in air pollution—and doing so without hurting the economy. More generally, President Bush has been right to insist that cost-benefit analysis, economic incentives, and sound science are necessary ingredients in sensible environmental policies.

Let's not be so terrified of the words "Social Security reform." If a degree of privatization can increase people's savings when they retire, so much the better. Rather than rejecting the President's reform proposals out of hand, let's work with him to make them better—to assure security for elderly Americans without necessarily freezing the system in its current form.

On these and other issues, bipartisan efforts would have big advantages. Most important, they would help to make American government work better for the American people. They would also devote both time and energy to the most promising proposals—and thus divert time and energy from the most unpromising and destructive ones. And they would establish the possibility of civility and cooperation, in a way that could pay some big dividends when the going gets tougher.

It's the Constitution, stupid. The last quarter-century has seen a determined, self-conscious, and highly-organized effort to reshape the federal judiciary—and hence to change the meaning of the Constitution. The effort has been astonishingly successful, producing a radical shift in a little over two decades. As a result of that shift—America's quiet revolution—what was considered conservative on the federal bench in 1980 is now considered moderate; what was then moderate is now liberal; what was then liberal is now absent; and what was then reactionary is now conservative (and entirely mainstream).

For most of this period, Democrats have put up only token resistance. But when President Bush and his allies speak of "strict construction," don't be fooled. That term is code for an approach that reads the Constitution as if it incorporates, on far too many issues, the views of the extreme right of the Republican Party. Liberals, moderates, and principled conservatives need to expose this cynical strategy for what it is—and to resist it through both words and deeds.

In the last few years, right-wing activists have become more ambitious than ever. There is a great deal of talk about restoration of the "Constitution in Exile"—the Constitution as it existed in 1932, before President Franklin Delano Roosevelt's New Deal. Under this Constitution, the powers of the national government were sharply limited. The National Labor Relations Act of 1935, not to mention the Civil Rights Act of 1964, would have been impermissible. Under the Constitution in Exile, racial discrimination was perfectly acceptable. The right to privacy did not exist. The really important right was freedom of contract, which threw minimum-wage and maximum-hour legislation into constitutional doubt. Many of President Bush's supporters, and some of his nominees, think that the Constitution of 1932 was the right one, and that it needs to be restored to power.

To be sure, the Supreme Court tends to move slowly, and even if President Bush is able to do whatever he wants, the Court would not adopt the Constitution of 1932; but it would certainly move in that direction. We should resist any effort by President Bush to appoint right-wing activists to the federal bench, and especially to the Supreme Court.

For many people, the most pressing issue is the fate of Roe v. Wade and women's right to choose. In 1992, the Rehnquist court cut back on the ruling but preserved its core, by a narrow 5-to-4 vote. New Bush appointments might well lead the court to return the issue to the states. More broadly, a newly constituted court would be unsympathetic to any claim that the Constitution protects sexual and reproductive privacy from state intervention. I certainly do not want the Court to overrule Roe v. Wade or to reject the right of privacy. But we need to make a distinction here. For too long, liberals have asked a lot of the federal courts; they have pushed many of their arguments before judges rather than before the people, and they've gotten into trouble for doing that. Principled conservatives have been right to object to liberal judicial activism. The most serious problem is that unprincipled conservatives, now able to dominate the federal bench, are promoting an activist agenda of their own—and calling it "strict construction."

If President Bush is able to appoint right-wing activists, the new court would likely strike down most campaign-finance reform. It would probably be inclined to invalidate parts of the Endangered Species Act and the Clean Water Act as beyond Congress' authority. It might well elevate commercial speech to the same status as political speech—thus forbidding controls on commercials by tobacco companies, among others. It would probably limit congressional efforts to protect disabled people, women, and the elderly from various forms of discrimination. More radically, it might interpret the Second Amendment so as to reduce the power of Congress and the states to enact gun-control legislation. This right-wing agenda for constitutional reform must be exposed and countered.

It's also opportunity and security. With what ideals should President Bush's most destructive proposals be opposed? The most important

Security:

president of the twentieth century, Franklin Delano Roosevelt, provided the best answer: *Opportunity and Security.* Consider a little history, from the last time that national security was threatened here at home.

On January 11, 1944, the United States was involved in its longest conflict since the Civil War. The war effort was going well, and Roosevelt wanted to focus on the highest principle. His State of the Union Address began by emphasizing that "the one supreme objective for the future"— for all nations—was captured "in one word: security." Roosevelt argued that the term "means not only physical security which provides safety from attacks by aggressors" but includes as well "economic security, social security, moral security." Roosevelt insisted that "essential to peace is a decent standard of living for all individual men and women and children in all nations. Freedom from fear is eternally linked with freedom from want."

As Roosevelt saw it, "necessitous men are not free men. " He echoed the words of the Declaration of Independence, urging a kind of Declaration of Interdependence: "In our day these economic truths have become accepted as self-evident. We have accepted, so to speak, a second Bill of Rights under which a new basis of security and prosperity can be established for all—regardless of station, race, or creed."

Then he listed the relevant rights:

New Rights 1944

"The right to a useful and remunerative job in the industries or shops or farms or mines of the Nation;

The right to earn enough to provide adequate food and clothing and recreation;

The right of every farmer to raise and sell his products at a return which will give him and his family a decent living;

The right of every businessman, large and small, to trade in an atmosphere of freedom from unfair competition and domination by monopolies at home or abroad;

The right of every family to a decent home;

The right to adequate medical care and the opportunity to achieve and enjoy good health;

The right to adequate protection from the economic fears of
old age, sickness, accident, and unemployment;
   The right to a good education."

Security at Home

"After this war is won," Roosevelt said, "we must be prepared to
move forward, in the implementation of these rights." And there was a
close connection between this implementation and the coming international order. "America's own rightful place in the world," he said,
"depends in large part upon how fully these and similar rights have been
carried into practice for our citizens. For unless there is security here at
home there cannot be lasting peace in the world."

Roosevelt's Second Bill of Rights was designed to protect the most fundamental of human interests: basic opportunity and minimal security. To
say the least, President Bush has failed to speak in these terms; and this has
been the most serious failure, and lost opportunity, of his presidency thus
far. After the attacks of September 11, a key disappointment of the Bush
administration has been its refusal to treat the risk of terrorism as a reason
for an appreciation of human vulnerability in all its forms. While constantly invoking both "liberty" and "security," the Bush administration has failed
to see that these ideals call not merely for protection against bullets and
bombs but also against hunger, disease, illiteracy, and desperate poverty.

Roosevelt, himself a victim of polio, believed that each of us is vulner-
able to dangers that cannot be wholly prevented in what he called this "man-
made" world of ours. In Roosevelt's words, "Government has a final responsibility for the well-being of its citizenship. If private co-operative endeavor
fails to provide work for willing hands and relief for the unfortunate, those
suffering hardship from no fault of their own have a right to call upon the
Government for aid; and a government worthy of its name must make fit-
ting response." Insofar as the Second Bill would ensure food, clothing, shelter, and health care for all, it would insure against the worst of those dangers. Americans need to recover Roosevelt's insistence on opportunity and
security, and to see these as preconditions for human freedom. Here, then,
is the core of a response to the worst of President Bush's programs.

opportunity & security

Two positive ideas here: Let's increase the Earned Income Tax Credit, which already lifts millions of people out of poverty, and helps to make work pay. And let's work hard for energy independence, in order to protect the environment, promote national security, and find avenues for creating new and better jobs.

Have fun. People are more likely to succeed, in politics and elsewhere, if they enjoy what they're doing. Franklin Delano Roosevelt, the most successful president in American history, loved his job, had a tremendous sense of humor, and disarmed his sharpest critics with jokes. ("You have heard," he once said to a large and skeptical audience, "that I am, at best, an ogre . . . and that I eat millionaires for breakfast.") President Bill Clinton obviously relished politics and running for president, and he liked to respond to harsh attacks with bemusement ("that dog won't hunt," he said to President George H.W. Bush); the same holds for Ronald Reagan ("There you go again," he said to Jimmy Carter). George W. Bush obviously didn't like the debates, and that hurt him; but he did seem to have a lot of fun at campaign events, and that helped him.

Compare Jimmy Carter, Michael Dukakis, George H.W. Bush, Al Gore, and John Kerry—diverse and honorable people, to be sure, but a relatively humorless group and not the most fun crowd, at least not on the campaign trail. John Kerry did many things right, but he would have been a better candidate if he had appeared to enjoy what he was doing, or proved able to make a few good jokes. (Quiz question: Why wasn't Theresa Heinz Kerry able to provide more help to her husband? Answer: She didn't like campaigning, and it showed.)

The next four years won't always be a ton of fun, but human beings have a remarkable capacity to enjoy themselves even in difficult times. A sense of fun is also contagious; it breeds more of the same. Let's work with President Bush on his good ideas, aggressively resist right-wing judicial activism, and work for both opportunity and security for all. If we do that, we might be able to have some fun during the President's second term—and make the country work a lot better in the process.

STANDING OUR GROUND IN THE FIGHT FOR JUSTICE AND A STRONG DEMOCRACY
JAMIN B. RASKIN

The great advantage to being marginalized is that, in the margins, you can find space to innovate.

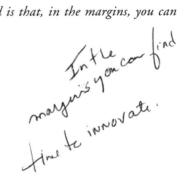

Jamin B. Raskin is a professor of constitutional law and the First Amendment at American University. He is the author of *Overruling Democracy: the Supreme Court versus the American People* and founded the Marshall-Brennan Constitutional Literacy Project, which sends gifted law students into public high schools to teach a course in constitutional literacy.

When I went down to see my sister and her family in Charlottesville before the election, crossing from blue Maryland into red Virginia, I saw a car pass by with a delightful bumper sticker that read, "If guns are outlawed, how am I going to shoot liberals?"

This triggered the memory of something Jesse Jackson once told me: "Rabbit hunting is a lot fun—until the rabbits start shooting back."

Well, I imagine liberal-hunting must be a lot of fun these days, too—and will continue to be until the liberals start shooting back.

That is no easy thing. By temperament, most of us are not big on shooting at other people—in the metaphorical, much less literal, sense. We don't trust violence to solve most conflicts. We don't believe that we need to humiliate and destroy our opponents to make political progress. We favor appeals to reason and moral sentiment over the imposition of power through the barrel of a gun. People know this about us. This is why a helmeted Governor Michael Dukakis looked ridiculous driving around in his big tank. This is why his once-Lieutenant Governor John Kerry, the only guy in the 2004 race who had actually *shot* enemy soldiers, looked comically forced and phony in his Deer Hunter camouflage hunting gear that suddenly appeared a few days before the election.

In truth, most liberals share the attitude shown by Atticus Finch, who refused to buy Jem a gun and would use his own rifle only to put a rabid dog out of its misery.

But remember this: Atticus was one hell of a shot when the occasion demanded it.

Indeed, this is the non-ersatz valor and courage of the liberal American, personified best by Franklin D. Roosevelt: a passionate and palpable love of peace and compassion for other people that is backed up by a ferocious determination to stare down and defeat fascist thuggery, racism, and religious bigotry at any cost.

I think of my Uncle Mel who flew dozens of bombing missions over Germany during World War II but, up until his death two years ago, bitterly opposed the lurid profiteering of the military-industrial complex and the dirty little wars of our national security apparatus.

cruelty

I think of George McGovern, another World War II flying hero who got pasted as a patsy and a wimp by that notorious coward and corrupt weakling Richard Nixon simply because he wanted to end the savagery of the Vietnam War.

The Republican propagandists did the same thing in 2004 to John Kerry, a decorated war hero, whose service was questioned and lambasted because he had the moral courage to oppose the war in Vietnam, whose horrors he had seen up close.

George W. Bush is in a long line of spoiled and smirking baby-boom right-wingers who used family influence to skip out of wartime military service but now demonize liberal veterans for threatening our security. In this topsy-turvy universe, "strong on defense" simply means "willing to risk untold thousands of other Americans' lives in order to kill as many hundreds of thousands of foreigners, military or civilian, as necessary in order to achieve whatever objective we proclaim at any given time, recalling that we will never be bound by the original reason given for entering a conflict."

The Republicans will get away with this arrogant trick until we sharply raise the political costs of their hypocrisy, folly and stupidity.

Now is the time for America's liberals to "stand in the place where you live," as REM has it, to rearm, reload and return rhetorical fire against the rampaging forces of right-wing power.

What will this mean concretely?

Of the human vices, as my beloved college professor Judith Shklar argued, liberals are traditionally most concerned to <u>stop cruelty</u>. This is why many advances in our history—the abolition of slavery, the spread of human rights doctrine—follow from liberal agitation. We wake up trying to figure out how to make the world a more humane place. We denounce dictators and human rights violations.

Conservatives, who claim to follow objective ethical codes based usually on religion, are obsessed with perceived sexual vices, especially the unpardonable sin of same-sex sodomy, and they are enraged by the liberal hypocrisy that surrounds them. They believe that it suffices to discredit an argument to show that its proponents are not living up to their own

Now is the time to stand in the place where you live.

professed ideals. They are driven crazy by the sexual hypocrisy of "family values" New Democrats like Bill Clinton and Chuck Robb and the perceived moral hypocrisy of "limousine liberals" like the Kennedys who try to redistribute wealth towards the working poor while themselves living the high life. (They prefer for the rich to be Cadillac conservatives and to act in concert to protect their class privilege.) They never get exercised by sexual hypocrisy on the Right, as exemplified by the lecherous and slightly deranged Bill O'Reilly or the President's married but adulterous brother who welcomed Japanese prostitutes into his hotel room as a delightful business gratuity or the sadistic, forced mass homosexual group sex acts paid for and staged by employees of the U.S. government at Abu Graib prison at the same time that conservatives mounted a huge campaign to fine CBS for fleetingly revealing Janet Jackson's left breast during the 2004 Super Bowl. They never turn on the moral hypocrites who are pervasive in their midst, like Republican operative Jack Abramoff, who made an art form out of shaking down Indian tribes for millions of dollars in lobbying fees to take care of regulatory problems that he secretly helped to create behind their backs, all the while squealing with delight over his own clients' stupidity.

Liberals rarely have the stomach for denouncing and exposing political hypocrisy, the rhetorical technique that is the very lifeblood of conservative talk radio and Karl Rove's Machiavellian-playbook campaigns. We understand that hypocrisy—failing to match our deeds and our words—is practically inevitable for human beings and may indeed be the price of having ideals in the first place. If you have no ideals and principles, hey—there's no chance of betraying them.

But the extraordinary depth of conservative hypocrisy today—and the relentless conservative assaults on alleged liberal hypocrisy—now make possible all kinds of unspeakable cruelties in the world and astounding injustices in our society. It may not be in our nature to point these things out, but we let the machinery of Republican hypocrisy go on at our own peril. We must have the toughness to blow the whistle on the lying, cheating, depraved corruption, religious extremism, ideological fanaticism, and horrible violence associated with the Right. And we have to pour shame on the people who participate in the vast money-and-war-making operation that is the Bush presidency. We cannot be meek for, as the great Ben Franklin said, "If you make yourself a sheep, the wolves will eat you."

And, yet, these are just day-to-day political and rhetorical tactics that could help us to climb back out of our hole. What are the prospects of actually moving America forward?

We begin with the recognition that, ever since the 2000 presidential election ended in grand theft (electoral), the essential structural safety valve of American government—the system of checks and balances—has broken down. James Madison's essential fear—the collapse of all institutional and political powers into one—has materialized. The Republican Party now controls the U.S. Senate, the U.S. House, the White House, the Supreme Court, practically every federal judicial circuit, a majority of the state governorships and legislatures, the lobbying establishment and large parts of corporate America. Moreover, the Republican Party itself has been captured by a fairly extreme right-wing faction that rolls over moderate Republicans, like the Chairman of the Senate Foreign Relations Committee, Richard Lugar and his colleague Chuck Hagel, who have expressed shock at the administration's lethal mismanagement of the Iraq invasion.

Furthermore, Republican leaders, who know how to do nothing better than manipulate the levers of power, have figured out how to program our antiquated political institutions to secure their lockdown of American government. With Karl Rove at the helm, Republican state legislatures have aggressively gerrymandered U.S. House districts to insulate their majority in the House, at one point acting so outrageously in Texas that Democratic legislators actually fled the state and hid in New Mexico in an act of legislative civil disobedience that, alas, proved futile. (The Bush administration used the federal government to track them down.) Rove's King Kong tactics and computerized matching of voters to politicians produced the ouster of four Democratic House incumbents in 2004.

At the same time, Republicans have mastered the conservative, Dixie-accented arithmetic of the Electoral College, which was born out of a fatal compromise with the slave masters from the small southern states like South Carolina and Alabama. They extracted not only the right to have the same number of U.S. senators as populous northern states like New York and Pennsylvania, but the right to count "three fifths" of their slaves for the purposes of congressional reapportionment, substantially inflating the numbers of white supremacists defending the "peculiar institution" in the U.S. House. The presidential Electoral College then reproduced and accentuated these mechanisms of disproportion by giving each state a number of presidential electors equal to its congressmen plus two for its Senators. These tricks worked like a dream: four out of our five first presidents were Virginia slave masters and the South has always played the Electoral College card in presidential elections. The Dixiecrat Democratic Party of the 20th century was, for a long period, the party of political white supremacy and when it began to evolve away from that primitivism, racists like Harry Byrd, Strom Thurmond and George Wallace left the party and ran for president as independents, removing dozens of Electoral College votes from the Democratic column and sending a sharp message about the political dangers of black civil rights. After he secured passage of the Voting Rights Act of 1965, LBJ correctly predicted that the Democrats would lose the white south for a generation, a prediction that proved to be both prescient and wildly optimistic.

Today, the beating heart of the Republican Party's Electoral College machine is the old Confederacy, which provided Bush a majority of his Electoral College votes. As the party of white backlash, the Republicans can count on a Solid South and may therefore spend their time developing federal policies in defense, intelligence, agriculture, industrial policy, trade protection, religious "charitable choice," and corporate welfare shrewdly targeted to buy off key swing constituencies in the handful of swing states. This was the successful ticket in 2004.

So what can we do beyond slamming the Republicans for their dangerous and extreme policies?

The great advantage to being marginalized is that, in the margins, you can find space to innovate. In the political wilderness, we can remake the way we practice politics and redesign our political institutions:

Expand and remake the Democratic Party by adding to its existing fundraising and campaign functions the social movement, social solidarity and social service functions we need. The old-fashioned Democratic Party, rooted in big-city political machines, used to deliver things to people: jobs, sidewalks, connections, a sense of belonging. Those days are over, but there are crying social needs from the bottom in America that, of the major parties, only the Democrats care about at all. Yet, our quadrennial campaign appeals for votes on issues like national health insurance ring hollow if there has not been a strong legislative push on these issues and if the Party itself has not done anything directly to help. We won't see any movement in Washington on national health care in the next four years, but the Democratic Party should organize a private national health insurance plan for uninsured people who cannot afford to wait for the next Democratic sweep of Congress. It could be capitalized initially by, say, 15% of all party contributions. With millions of dollars in political money to launch it and back it up, this plan could be a real solution for uninsured families, and it would send a dramatic signal to America about which side the Democratic Party is really on—and not just rhetorically. After hundreds of millions of dollars were spent on the Kerry campaign in 2004, both inside and out, what do we have to show for it today? Had we taken even just $10 million to launch a Democratic Health Insurance Plan, Democrats would have concretely helped a lot of fellow Americans and built a far more enduring political legacy. Similarly, working families are having a very tough time pulling money together for college tuition. If we took 10% of all money raised in party contributions and created a Democratic Scholarship and Loan Fund to send young Democrats to college, again we would be putting our money where our mouths are and scoring all kinds of political points at the same time. Since the Democrats are the party of labor, we should also create a Democratic Strike Fund to help workers and their families make it through workplace conflicts.

The point is that we have to stop replicating a model of the Democratic Party as an empty vessel for fundraising that takes hundreds of millions of dollars from progressive people and unions at election time to give to broadcast corporations and millionaire political consultants.

Turn America's powerful new progressive networks towards the young population, the swing states and local problems. The awesome power of the liberal mobilization in 2004—so strong it almost defeated an incumbent president in wartime—came not from the Democratic National Committee or the Kerry-Edwards ticket but rather from progressive civil society: the labor unions, America Coming Together, the Center for American Progress, Mothers Opposed to Bush, the Nation magazine, and MoveOn.org, to name just a few. These networks need to turn their attention now to the key winnable swing states: Ohio, Florida, Iowa, Nevada, New Mexico, New Hampshire. Right now we should start to set up think tanks, voter registration drives, summer camps, national conferences and conventions in these states. The progressive movement cannot win if it is a bunch of bureaucracies in Washington. Similarly, these networks need to target young people by generating local community service projects and cultural events that will attract them. Why not put the Vote for Change rock musicians back on the road but link their concerts to mass political and civic action such as literacy drives, housing construction, and resource mobilization for schools?

Build a campaign for constitutional defense and reconstruction and political renewal in America. The Rehnquist Court has been undermining and shrinking our Constitution, an already flawed document originally conceived to govern a slave Republic of Christian white male property-owners. But the glory of our Constitutional development has been its progressive amendment to expand the circle of democratic community and the rights of the people. We need to revive constitutional dialogue and change, beginning with an amendment to guarantee universal suffrage and the right of every American citizen to vote and be represented at every level of government.

The Rehnquist Court has denied and eroded our basic political rights: we have more than 8 million disenfranchised Americans today, from vote-less citizens living in Puerto Rico and other federal territories to more than a half-million citizens in Washington D.C, the only national capital on earth whose residents lack voting representation in the national legislature, to more than five million citizens all over America who have lost the franchise because of criminal convictions. It is time to make "one person one vote" a reality. And we need to confront the miserable failure of winner-take-all elections, which leave huge numbers of Americans without meaningful political representation. San Francisco has pointed the way with its embrace of instant runoff voting, but liberals need to be far more proactive and flexible in suggesting new voting technologies and techniques.

Furthermore, the Electoral College has frozen American politics, giving disproportionate power to southern and conservative rural interests, depressing participation as people recognize the uselessness of voting in most states, and dividing the country along sectional lines. We should adopt direct majority election of the president like the rest of the democratic world and make every American's vote count.

Similarly, in the face of the Court's ruling that there is no fundamental right to a public education and that states may have school systems in which children in one county or district have twice as much money spent on their educations as in others, we need a constitutional amendment guaranteeing students the right to an equally funded excellent public education. This reform is as critical to meaningful political democracy as the right to vote.

The place to start is with the young: educating them about the Constitution, the struggle for its expansion during and after the Civil War, and the need to transform it again. We also need to teach them the Jeffersonian conception of a wall of separation between church and state, a vision that has been overrun by "charitable choice" and Republican efforts to steer public money into church-run entities.

Back at the end of the 18th century, when another conservative government took over and drove the country towards foreign hostilities while clamping down on immigration and political dissent at home, Thomas Jefferson assured his friends that the "reign of witches" would "pass over, their spells dissolve, and the people, recovering their true sight," would "restore their government to its true principles."

We have to show some Jeffersonian patience at this despondent moment. For, as in Jefferson's time, "we are suffering deeply in spirit, and incurring the horrors of a war and long oppressions of enormous public debt." And yet we can be sure that, if we stand our ground and keep fighting hard for the principles of justice and democracy that unite us, our luck will turn and, as Jefferson forecast, "we shall have an opportunity of winning back the principles we have lost."

VOTING & ELECTION REFORM

KERRY WON
GREG PALAST

Our betters in the political and media elite have told us to get over it, move on. But where do we move to? What's on the other side when we "get over" democracy?

Greg Palast is the author of *The Best Democracy Money Can Buy*. He is a frequent contributor to *Harper's Magazine*, for whom he investigated the vote. He has also investigated the Bush administration for the British newspaper *The Guardian*, and for BBC Television's *Newsnight*.

I know you don't want to hear it. You can't face one more hung chad. But I don't have a choice. As a journalist examining that messy sausage called American democracy, it's my job to tell you who got the most votes on November 2, 2004. In Ohio and New Mexico, it was John Kerry.

Really, no foolin'.

Most voters in Ohio thought they were voting for Kerry. In the wee hours of the morning after the election, CNN's exit poll showed Kerry beating Bush among Ohio women by 53 percent to 47 percent. Kerry also defeated Bush among Ohio's male voters 51 percent to 49 percent. Unless a third gender voted in Ohio, Kerry took the state.

So what's going on here? Answer: the exit polls are accurate. Pollsters ask, "Who did you vote for?" Unfortunately, they don't ask the crucial, question, "Was your vote counted?" The voters don't know.

Here's why. Although the exit polls show that most voters in Ohio punched cards for Kerry-Edwards, thousands of these votes were simply not recorded. This was predictable and it was predicted.

Once again, at the heart of the Ohio uncounted vote game are, I'm sorry to report, hanging chads and pregnant chads, plus some other ballot tricks old and new.

The election in Ohio was not decided by the voters but by something called "spoilage." Typically in the United States, about 3 percent of the vote is voided, just thrown away, not recorded. When the bobble-head boobs on the tube tell you Ohio or any state was won by 51 percent to 49 percent, don't you believe it... it has never happened in the United States, because the total never reaches a neat 100 percent. The television totals simply subtract out the spoiled vote.

Whose Votes Are Discarded?

And not all votes spoil equally. According to the brutal statistics tucked away in the unread reports of the U.S. Civil Rights Commission and Harvard Law School's Civil Rights Project, of the *two million* votes spoiled in a typical presidential electio, more than half come from African-American precincts. In other words, about one million black votes simply *vanish,* chucked into the dumpster.

We saw this in Florida in 2000. Exit polls showed Gore with a plurality of at least 50,000, but it didn't match the official count. That's because the official, Secretary of State Katherine Harris, excluded 179,855 spoiled votes. In Florida, as in Ohio, most of these votes lost were cast on punch cards where the hole wasn't punched through completely—leaving a 'hanging chad,'—or was punched extra times. Whose cards were discarded?

Civil Rights Commission and Harvard team statisticians went through the pile of ballots in the dumpster and calculated that 54% of those discards ballots were cast by black folks. Your chance a vote-counting machine will "reject" your ballot depends on your skin color. A Black citizen of Florida is 900% more likely to have their ballot tossed out on a technicality than a white one.

The sorry truth is that Florida is terribly typical. That horrid ratio holds nationwide.

So here we go again. Or, here we *don't* go again. Because unlike last time, Democrats didn't even ask Ohio to conduct a hand count of these punch cards with the not-quite-punched holes (called "under-votes" in the voting biz). Nor are they demanding we look at the "over-votes" where voter intent may be discerned.

Ohio is one of the last states in America to still use the vote-spoiling punch-card machines. And the Secretary of State of Ohio, J. Kenneth Blackwell, wrote before the election, "the possibility of a close election with punch cards as the state's primary voting device invites a Florida-like calamity."

Blackwell, a rabidly partisan Republican, warmed up to the result of sticking with machines that have a habit of eating Democratic votes.

When asked if he feared being this year's Katherine Harris, the politically ambitious Secretary of State said, "Last time I checked, Katherine Harris wasn't in a soup line, she's in Congress."

In Ohio, 93,000 votes were spoiled. According to studies of the top voting demographer in Ohio, Mark Salling of Cleveland State University, the match between votes spoiled and African-American precincts is "overwhelming."

"Provisional Voting"—Jim Crow's Back-Of-The-Bus Ballots

Add to the spoiled ballots a second group of uncounted votes, the 'provisional' ballots, and—*voila!*—the White House would have turned Democrat blue.

But that won't happen because of the peculiar way provisional ballots are counted or, more often, *not* counted. Introduced nationally by federal law in 2002, the provisional ballot was designed especially for voters of color. Proposed by the Congressional Black Caucus to save the rights of those wrongly scrubbed from voter rolls, it was, in Republican-controlled swing states, twisted into a back-of-the-bus ballot unlikely to be tallied.

Unlike the real thing, these ballots are counted only by the whimsy and rules of a state's top elections official; and in Ohio, that gives a virtual ballot veto to Bush-Cheney campaign co-chair, Blackwell.

Mr. Blackwell has a few rules to make sure a large proportion of provisional ballots won't be counted. For the first time in memory, the Secretary of State has banned counting ballots cast in the "wrong" precinct, though all neighborhoods share the same President.

Over 155,000 Ohio voters were shunted to these second-class ballots. The election-shifting bulge in provisional ballots (more than 3% of the electorate) was the direct result of the national Republican strategy that targeted African-American precincts for mass challenges on Election Day.

This is the first time in four decades that a political party has systematically barred—in this case successfully—hundreds of thousands of Black voters from access to the voting booth. While investigating for BBC Television, we obtained three dozen of the Republican Party's confidential "caging" lists, their title for spreadsheets listing names and addresses of voters they intended to block on any pretext.

We found that every single address of the thousands on these Republican hit lists was located in Black-majority precincts. You might find that nasty and racist. It may also be a crime.

Before 1965, Jim Crow laws in the Deep South did not bar Blacks from voting. Rather, the segregationist game was played by applying minor technical voting requirements only to African-Americans.

That year, Congress voted to make profiling and impeding minority voters, even with a legal pretext, a criminal offence under the Voting Rights Act.

But that didn't stop the Republicans of '04. Their legally questionable mass challenge to Black voters is not some low-level dirty tricks operation of local party hacks. Emails we obtained show the lists were copied directly to the Republican National Committee's chief of research and to the director of a state campaign.

Many challenges center on changes of address. On one Republican caging list, 50 addresses changed from Jacksonville to overseas, African-American soldiers shipped "Over There."

You don't have to guess the preferences registered on the provisional ballots. Republicans went on a challenging rampage, while Democrats pledged to hold to the tradition of letting voters vote.

Blackwell has said he counted all the "valid" provisional ballots. However, his rigid regulations, like the new guess-your-precinct rule, were rigged to knock out enough voters to keep Bush's skinny lead alive.

Other pre-election maneuvers by state and local Republican officials—late and improbably large purges of voter rolls, rejection of registrations—maximized the use of provisional ballots which will never be counted. For example, a voter wrongly tagged as an ineligible "felon" voter (and there's plenty in that category, mostly African-Americans), will lose their ballot even though they are wrongly identified.

Bush, according to the networks, "won" by 136,483 votes in Ohio... before any attempt to hand-count the spoiled ballots; before anyone counted a single provisional ballot. Count them up and the totals begin to match the exit polls; and, golly, you've got yourself a new president.

Enchanted State's Enchanted Vote

Now, on to New Mexico, where a Kerry plurality—if all votes are counted—is more obvious still. *Before* the election, in TomPaine.com, I wrote, "John Kerry is down by several thousand votes in New Mexico, though not one ballot has yet been counted."

How did that happen? It's the spoilage, stupid; and the provisional ballots.

CNN said George Bush took New Mexico by 11,620 votes. Again, the network total added up to that miraculous, and non-existent, '100 percent' of ballots cast.

New Mexico reported in the last race a spoilage rate of 2.68 percent, votes lost almost entirely in Hispanic, Native American and poor precincts—Democratic turf. From the November 2 vote, assuming the same ballot-loss rate, we can expect to see 18,000 ballots in the spoilage bin.

Spoilage has a very Democratic look in New Mexico. Hispanic voters in the Enchanted State, who voted more than two to one for Kerry, are five times as likely to have their vote spoil as a white voter. Counting these uncounted votes would easily overtake the Bush 'plurality.'

Already, the election-bending effects of spoilage are popping up in the election stats, exactly where we'd expect them: in heavily Hispanic areas controlled by Republican elections officials. Chaves County, in the "Little Texas" area of New Mexico, has a 44 percent Hispanic population, plus African Americans and Native Americans, yet George Bush "won" there 68 percent to 31 percent.

I spoke with Chaves' Republican county clerk before the election, and he told me that this huge spoilage rate among Hispanics simply indicated that such people simply can't make up their minds on the choice of candidate for president. Oddly, these brown people drive across the desert to register their indecision in a voting booth.

Now, let's add in the effect on the New Mexico tally of provisional ballots.

"They were handing them out like candy," Albuquerque journalist Renee Blake reported of provisional ballots. Over 20,000 were given out. Who got them?

Santiago Juarez who ran the "Faithful Citizenship" program for the Catholic Archdiocese in New Mexico, told me that "his" voters, poor Hispanics, whom he identified as solid Kerry supporters, were handed the iffy provisional ballots. Hispanics were given provisional ballots, rather than the countable kind "almost religiously," he said, at polling stations when there was the least question about a voter's identification. Some voters, Santiago said, were simply turned away.

Kerry Blacks Out

Some crackpot writer in Salon.com claimed he had absolute proof the vote count in Ohio wasn't bent: "Kerry conceded."

Kerry's diving to the mat tells us only that he and his advisors understood the cold calculus against taking the fight to the end. To count the ballots, Kerry's lawyers would, first, have to demand a hand reading of the punch cards. Blackwell, armed with the Supreme Court's *Bush v. Gore* diktat, would undoubtedly pull a "Kate Harris" by halting or restricting a hand count. Most daunting, Kerry's team would also, as one state attorney general pointed out to me, have to litigate each and every rejected provisional ballot in court. This would entail locating up to a hundred thousand voters to testify to their right to the vote, with Blackwell challenging each with a holster full of regulations from the old Jim Crow handbook.

Given the odds and the cost to his political career, Kerry bent, not to the will of the people, but to the will to power of the Ohio Republican machine. I can understand it, but I can't applaud it.

It was heartening that, during his campaign, John Kerry broke the political omerta that seems to prohibit public mention of the color of votes not counted in America. "Don't tell us that in the strongest democracy on earth a million disenfranchised African Americans is the best we can do." The Senator promised the NAACP convention, "This November, we're going to make sure that every single vote is counted."

But then Kerry became the first presidential candidate in history to break a campaign promise after *losing* an election. The Senator waited less than 24 hours to abandon more than a quarter million Ohio voters still waiting for their provisional and chad-spoiled ballots to be counted.

"Get Over It"? Not Me.

We have yet to total here the votes lost in missing absentee ballots, in eyebrow-raising touch screen tallies, in purges of legal voters from registries and other games played in swing states. Kerry won, so hold your victory party. But make sure the shades are down: it may become illegal to demand a full vote count under PATRIOT Act III.

Why dwell on these things? Our betters in the political and media elite have told us to get over it, move on.

But where do we move *to*? What's on the other side when we "get over" democracy?

If there's a point to this piece it is that America still maintains a segregated Apartheid voting system. Black, Hispanic and Native-American voters are the immediate targets, but all Americans dispossessed by the system are the victims—those without jobs, without health insurance, without decent schools... you know the list. As the demographer Phil Klinkner pointed out, it was the rich, those with incomes over $100,000 a year, who provided George Bush with his margin of victory over the rest of us.

I say, "over the rest of us," because Bush did more than defeat a candidate named Kerry, he defeated the voters, not just through ballot manipulations but through a billion-dollar avalanche of purchased advertising and PR disinformation. We the people were defeated because our government was turned into a profit-center to generate returns for those donors who paid for this electoral class war.

Here's an idea. It's time for a new Civil Rights movement, a Democracy Movement. In the Fifties and Sixties, Martin Luther King led nationwide protests to force the government to give all Americans, in particular African Americans, the right to vote. Unfortunately, we won the right to vote but not to have those votes *counted*.

Democracy, the vote, must be our demand. Again.

—Oliver Shykles and Matthew Pascarella contributed to this report.

REVIVING AMERICAN DEMOCRACY
HOWARD DEAN

If you want your country back, you have to take it back. Believe me—the right-wingers aren't going to be nice about giving it back.

Howard Dean was governor of Vermont from 1991 to 2003. He campaigned for the Democratic nomination in the 2004 presidential election, and is currently honorary chairman of Democracy for America, an organization dedicated to building a grassroots network for the Democratic party. He is the author of *You Have the Power: How to Take Back Our Country and Restore Democracy in America.*

Americans are a people unique in the world for their optimism, their faith, their ability to hope, and their belief that they can control their own fates. We are a relatively young country, uncynical by international standards, and though we've often been labeled by others as naïve, our capacity for hope and faith and optimism has also made us a magnet for people seeking hope and faith and control over their lives from all over the globe.

It horrifies me to see this strength of ours being squandered. It saddens me immeasurably to see the American spirit bending under the load of nonsense that passes for politics. It frightens me, too. I truly believe that much of America's power in the world comes from the fact that for so long, we've been able to inspire dreams of a better future in people around the world. Our source of power has been not our ability to bomb whole cities into oblivion, but our ability to peacefully captivate people's hearts and minds. It seemed to me that if we were failing to generate this power at home, then there was no way we could continue to do so overseas. The result was that we were seriously at risk of becoming a weak, second-rate nation.

We now face four more years of a Republican hard-right-dominated White House. By the time George W. Bush leaves office, he will have filled the benches up and down our judicial system with radical right-wing appointees. That means we will not see anything vaguely resembling positive change or democratic restoration for the foreseeable future. For at least another generation, we will not see anything resembling the America that so many of us know, and love, and miss.

Who can stop that from happening? You can. We all can. And only we can.

One of the first issues we need to address if we're going to get out the vote at a level required by a truly participatory democracy is the lack of excitement many people feel for the candidates put forth by our parties. Right now, in primaries, and in general elections where there's a third-party candidate, a fair number of voters feel forced to choose the candidate they think is viable. In the end, if they really want to defeat the opposition, they choose the candidate they think is most likely to do so, without enthusiasm and without much pride. As they often put it, they feel as if they're choosing the lesser of two evils. A population that feels like this is not going to be very motivated to vote.

One way to overcome this problem is by changing our voting system so that people can vote for candidates they believe in without risking the kind of outcome we saw in 2000 when third-party candidate Ralph Nader drew enough votes from Al Gore to ensure President Bush's Electoral College win. Other countries do this through a multi-party system that rules by coalition. We can do it in America by bringing in a new voting system that allows coalitions to be built *as you vote*. It's called instant runoff voting.

Instant runoff voting is a system in which you vote by ranking two or three candidates in order of preference. When the votes are tallied, if your top choice gets knocked out of the running, your vote reverts to your number two, and so on. It's like having a runoff election, only you don't need two elections to do it. This system, which has attracted the interest of a number of reform-minded people around the United States, is already in use in Europe and in city council elections in Cambridge, Massachusetts. Instant runoff voting was successful in San Francisco on Nov. 2. Although

there were some minor glitches, I suspect they will keep using it.

By way of illustration: Had we used instant runoff voting in 2000, most Nader supporters would have gone to the polls and voted for Ralph Nader first and Al Gore second. Since Nader, in the three-way tally afterward, wouldn't have finished in one of the top two slots, Al Gore would have been the beneficiary of roughly 60 percent of his votes and would have been chosen as the next president of the United States. (Most of Pat Buchanan's votes most likely would have gone to President Bush.)

Instant runoff voting would be beneficial for our electoral process, because it would encourage candidates to hold a firm set of principles without worrying that their beliefs could make them unviable. It would allow people to vote for candidates they really want to elect, thereby increasing both enthusiasm and turnout.

Still, it's important to remember: *Politicians can't solve our problems for us.*

One of the things wrong with our democracy right now is that people have been searching for someone to come along and unlock the door to a better future, make everyone feel better again, and heal what ails our country.

The truth is, that person is you, not me or any other politician or leader.

Thus, of all the initiatives I could mention, the most vital by far is the most simple: people taking power into their own hands, standing up, speaking out, and showing up in large enough number to effect change. Public involvement and grassroots activism—bringing reform to every level of the political food chain, from school board seats on up—that's how change will happen in America.

Voting is not enough.

Like most public officials, I've been to hundreds of schools and colleges over the years, exhorting young people to vote. I don't do that anymore. In my mind, voting gets you a D if you want to live in a healthy democracy. If you want an A, you have to vote. *And* you have to work in a campaign for a candidate for any office three hours a week. *And* you have to send your favorite candidate five or ten or fifty dollars. (Dean for America showed that many small donations can add up to $53 million pretty fast.) To get an A+, you have to run for office yourself. Run for the school board, county supervisor, state legislature, Congress. Run for student council or library trustee. If ordinary Americans like you don't run, people from the right wing or the Christian Coalition will. That's how we got where we are now.

If you want your country back, you have to take it back. Believe me—the right-wingers aren't going to be nice about giving it back.

We have a tendency to believe that history corrects itself—that if the political pendulum swings too far in any one direction, it will sooner or later swing back and settle somewhere in the middle thanks to the basic solidity of our institutions and the commonsense decency of our people.

There's some historical truth to that, but it's not going to happen now simply because it's a historical trend. It will happen if people like you use their power—the power they have in themselves, and the power they get by being part of a community—to make change.

IT'S THE DEMOCRACY, STUPID
DONNA BRAZILE

Before the sun goes down on this past election—before it becomes but an interesting chapter in our history—it is the responsibility of our elected officials and citizens' groups to channel the frustration from November 2 into positive energy to revive American democracy and give every citizen a voice at the political table. That is our new mission.

Donna Brazile is Chair of the Democratic National Committee's Voting Rights Institute and former campaign Manager for Al Gore 2000. She is also author of *Cooking with Grease: Stirring the Pots in American Politics*.

The 2004 presidential election raised grave concerns about the fundamental rights of Americans to vote, to have those votes counted, and to have the results actually reflect the will of the people. To rephrase that old Democratic campaign battle cry; "It's the Democracy, Stupid."

Although leading Democrats, including myself, fought hard to clean up the electoral mess from the 2000 election fiasco in Florida, voter intimidation and suppression resurfaced (especially among student voters, elderly voters, minorities and first time voters); voters were forced to wait in long lines, up to 14 hours in certain precincts; some polls did not open on time and other precincts ran out of ballots; there was confusion over the use of provisional ballots, the failure to deliver absentee ballots in a timely fashion, erroneous purging of legally registered voters from voter rolls, and questionable scrutiny of voter registration affidavits. Problems with voting equipment slowed the election process in some precincts and miscalculated votes in others.

Recent speculation concerning electronic vote tampering during the 2004 general election has ripened into litigation in Florida and Ohio and, as I write, the Government Accountability Office (GAO) has just announced its intention to examine the security and accuracy of voting technologies, distribution and allocation of voting machines, and counting of provisional ballots for the 2004 Presidential election. While the GAO's investigation is unlikely to change the outcome, the decision to examine various flaws in the 2004 general election is justified and warranted.

For example, some 57,000 complaints were filed with the Department of Justice and tens of thousand of phone calls were received by various civil rights groups on Election Day. The petition to seek an investigation by GAO was signed by six Democratic members of congress. In the words of the GAO: "The core principle of any democracy is the consent of the governed. All Americans, no matter how they voted, need to have confidence that when they cast their ballot, their voice is heard."

Inadequate regulation concerning the sanctity of our votes is inexcusable. Major efforts made in the business community to keep online and electronic transactions secure are well documented. The banking industry is committed to providing electronic and online security; the Gambling industry is committed to providing electronic security. Why are our deposits safer than our votes? Why are our bets safer than our ballots? Is preventing a fix on the Super Bowl odds more important than preventing a fix of an election? Why are ATM's and slot machines more secure than voting machines? Why on Earth? Does anyone think for one moment that the SEC would allow trading for a corporation that did not preserve the financial records essential for conducting a full audit? How could our legislators fail to provide logical regulatory safeguards to ensure the absence of vote tampering and require a paper trail for all electronic votes cast?

The late President Lyndon Johnson, who signed into law the 1965 Voting Rights Act, is credited with saying, "Voting is the life blood of our democracy." The right to vote and the right to have that vote counted are vital to Democracy because a vote represents a choice and our choice is the basis of freedom. Without a recognized vote there is no choice and without choice there is no freedom. Without freedom, there is no effective means to mandate and discern truth and integrity in government.

Before Freedom marched in Afghanistan and Iraq, it advanced through Montgomery and Selma. We can never take the right to vote for granted. Thomas Jefferson once said, "The price of freedom is eternal vigilance." Thomas Jefferson was right. So how is freedom doing on our own watch, here in the cradle of Liberty? If freedom is on the march, as President George W. Bush is fond of saying, why are people waiting in lines for four, six, fourteen hours to cast their ballots in a general election?

If freedom is on the march, why are young adults, the future leaders of our nation being dissuaded and prevented from registering to vote? If freedom is on the march, why are the ballots of our service men and women serving abroad not processed in a timely and effective manner? If freedom is on the march, why are our newest citizens scrutinized at the polls? Why are outdated and flawed voting machines serving as a substitute for the voice of the American electorate? Why aren't our legislators protecting our most powerful freedom? If having a voice in the election of our nation's leaders is the lifeblood of our democracy, why do our citizens continue to accept the inequities that have supported the inept power structures of modern U. S. culture?

The 1998 Higher Education Act requires that Colleges and Universities help students register to vote as a condition of receiving federal funding. A study recently completed by Harvard Institute of Politics and the Chronicle of Higher Education found that only 17% were in full compliance under the Act and more than one-third of colleges and universities do not comply with the Act's requirements. Many students have reported challenges from local officials when trying to register to vote despite the fact that in 1979 the U.S. Supreme Court confirmed that college students have the right to claim their campus address as their permanent address for purposes of voter registration.

Political tension, partisanship, discrimination and regulatory uncertainty have operated so as to frustrate attempts by many of our nation's eligible young adults to exercise their right and their duty to vote. Presumably, increasing the number of young voters will positively affect voter turnout in the future; and conversely, preventing young voters from exercising their right to vote will discourage civic participation in the future.

It's time we do more than whine and complain. The next round of Election Reform must include some relief to young adults to remove the artificial and illegal barriers that prevents them from fully exercising their right to vote. One area of reform that should be encouraged universally is early voting.

Voters in Florida of every race and means, young and elderly, healthy and disabled, eager to take advantage of early voting opportunities, stood in line for hours on end, battling sweltering heat and humidity and the occasional thunderstorm. I visited Orlando, Florida the weekend before Election Day where hundreds of people in low-income areas waited in hot, humid weather to cast their votes. The lines were three hours long. We commissioned an ice cream vendor to distribute a refreshing snack to the multitudes as they humbly waited to exercise their most precious freedom.

There were reports of voter registration irregularities ranging from destroying voter registration affidavits in Las Vegas, Nevada to inducing people to sign "petitions" that were, in actuality, partisan voter registration affidavits. Elderly Democrats in several Eastern states received phone calls informing them that they no longer had the right to vote.

Pennsylvania Democrats (most of them minorities or elderly voters) were fraudulently informed that due to heavy voter turnout, there had been an extension of the deadline and they could vote on Wednesday (November 3). Although the Republican Party denied any involvement in using suppression tactics, some of their officials were willing to speak the truth.

Last Summer, Michigan State Representative John Pappageorge (R-Troy) was quoted in the *Detroit Free Press* as saying, "If we do not suppress the Detroit vote, we're going to have a tough time in the election." African Americans comprise roughly 83% of Detroit's population. Again and again, Democratic members of Congress called on Attorney General John Ashcroft to investigate potential civil rights violations in the Orlando, Florida area where armed, plainclothes State law enforcement officers were questioning elderly black voters in their homes concerning absentee voting irregularities in the 2003 mayoral election. Critics claim that the tactics used by law enforcement officials have intimidated black voters and could suppress the vote during the 2004 general election.

This is but the latest in a series of historical attempts at voter suppression, primarily among minority, poor and young voters. In Kentucky in July 2004, African American Republicans joined together to request that their GOP State chairman renounce plans to place "vote challengers" in predominantly black precincts during the 2004 election cycle.

Voter fraud and voter intimidation is not limited to the South. In Multnomah County, Oregon, Republicans attempted to set aside the ballots of first-time voters who failed to produce identification at the time they voted despite the fact that Oregon requires no identification as a condition of voting. In South Dakota's 2004 primary, Native American registered voters were deprived of exercising their right to cast a ballot because they failed to produce photo identification at the polls, despite the fact that identification is not required under South Dakota law. This is why we must act now before our voting system is completely dysfunctional.

In the days following Senator John Kerry's concession speech, I urged Terry McAuliffe, Chair of the Democratic National Committee (DNC), to issue a letter to all Secretaries of State, requesting that they explicitly outline the standards and timelines that will be used to count the remaining votes. Three weeks after the request, the DNC had heard back from only two Secretaries of State (for Arizona and Kansas, respectively), who responded that all votes cast in those two states had been counted and were public information. Once again, this too is an area that calls for reform. Citizens should have access to the process and standards used to count all the votes. But, sadly, most of our Secretaries of States are partisan officials who bend over backwards to side with their own team. Still, we must hold them accountable.

Over my years spent crossing America organizing marches and countless voter registration drives, and my professional work advising politicians and political candidates, I have never forgotten a lesson that Martin Luther King put so well: "Voting is more than a badge of citizenship and dignity," he said, "it is an effective tool for change". It's time for change because that tool lies blunted, in part through neglect by our national leaders.

The Election Assistance Commission that was supposed to develop standards for voting and resources for implementing those standards has been under funded and understaffed. While certain election protection issues are under the control of the government, I believe that, as citizens, we can impact others. We can and we must demand that our legislators at the local, state and national levels make election reform a major policy priority. It is not enough to appoint commissions; there must be adequate funding for the commissions to be effective and there must be accountability, not just to Congress or to State and local legislators. There must be accountability to the voters of America. When it comes to voting in America, we can do better. We just have to want it badly enough.

Before the sun goes down on this past election—before it becomes but an interesting chapter in our history—it is the responsibility of our elected officials and citizens' groups to channel the frustration from November 2 into positive energy to revive American democracy and give every citizen a voice at the political table. That is our new mission, and it has not been accomplished.

Our work is incomplete. It is not time to grow weary. We must eagerly roll up our sleeves and fight for the most precious of our freedoms; we must persistently demand that incidents of election fraud be prosecuted to the full extent of the law. Systematic plots to deprive fellow Americans from exercising their valuable right to vote increasingly are accepted as politics as usual. It's time we demand answers to find out why there were long lines on Election Day.

Why did some precincts where voter registration is heavily weighted in favor of the opposition party have less machines and ballots than others? Did anyone interfere with voter registration applications? Were some voters intentionally misled to show up at the wrong precinct? In all these cases, what we are saying is, someone is tampering with citizen's right to vote and participate in the political process. As citizens, we must all demand an immediate assessment of what went wrong at the ballot box and work even harder to improve our electoral democracy.

All I know after a year of being on the frontlines to increase voter participation is we owe it to future generations to clean up our voting process. There is no place in our democracy for long lines, chads, malfunctioning voting machines and unnecessary barriers to keep people from voting and have their votes properly counted and recorded.

It is not easy to calculate the damages sustained as the result of election fraud, voter suppression and intimidation. The price we pay for corruption in government, abuse of power, the theft of one's basic freedom, complacency and apathy is dear indeed. To honor the legacy of the generations of Americans who constantly pushed us to realize America's full promise as a democracy, we must take up this fight. All Americans—irrespective of their party—must join in repairing the machine of our democracy and the heart of our nation. The battle continues.

THE MEDIA

RECLAIMING THE MEDIA FOR A
PROGRESSIVE FEMINIST FUTURE
JENNIFER L. POZNER

The progressive community must build a well-funded, populist movement for media reform by taking on the institutional and structural biases of today's media.

Jennifer L. Pozner is the founder and director of Women In Media & News (WIMN), a media analysis, training and advocacy organization. Her work has been published in *Ms.*, *Bitch*, *Newsday*, *Chicago Tribune*, and on AlterNet.org.

In April, 2004, more than one million protesters attended the "March for Women's Lives" to support a feminist agenda on reproductive rights, health care, violence against women, poverty, global affairs and more, making it the largest demonstration in Washington D.C. history.

Faced with a women's rights demo bigger than any 1960's civil rights or anti-war march, American media responded with a whimper, undercounting the marchers' numbers (citing "thousands" or "hundreds of thousands" instead of "more than a million") and underestimating the protesters' political significance, keeping the story in the news cycle typically for just one day . . . if that. *Time* magazine, which infamously declared feminism "dead" in a 1998 cover story, ignored the march entirely. Outlets like *Newsday,* Fox News and CNN played bait-and-switch, covering the march as an excuse to highlight a few hundred anti-abortion counter-protesters, as if their minute presence was equal in size and newsworthiness. Amid the largest gathering of female leaders, activists, academics and professionals in the history of the United States, the *Baltimore Sun* gave the first three quotes of their women's rights protest story to men. Even the *Washington Post's* Hank Stuever, who wrote one of the only pieces addressing the broad range of concerns raised at the march, couldn't help trivializing the women themselves, writing, "This is what a feminist looks like: Like a Powerpuff Girl went to college and got tattoos and somehow managed to keep great skin."

Overall, media implied that the demonstration would have little impact on the presidential race, never acknowledging that their dismissive coverage might lead the public to believe that women's rights are irrelevant during an election year.

How did we get here? After the election, seasoned activists and apolitical liberals alike began asking how Bush could have hoodwinked so many low-income, minority and women voters into supporting a corporate-welfare supporting, job squandering, sex-ed slashing, racial profiling, archconservative administration. Most of the theories bandied about— *Karl Rove out-organized us! Kerry forgot his antiwar roots!*—were certainly factors, but they miss the bigger picture. More important than any single botched campaign strategy is the overarching failure of the left to understand the role corporate media plays in shaping public opinion, public policy and, ultimately, political leadership.

To move forward in the next four years and beyond, the progressive community must build a well-funded, populist movement for media reform by taking on the institutional and structural biases of today's media. Right wing foundations have strategically invested in media over the past three decades in an effort to frame the public debate on their own terms. To that end, they've trained student journalists, funded conservative student newspapers, and funneled millions into right wing think tanks that pump out anti-feminist books, press releases, pundits and documentaries.

At the same time, as documented in Susan Faludi's 1991 manifesto *Backlash: The Undeclared War Against American Women,* the right used the media to stage a strategic "coup by euphemism," re-labeling rabid opposition to women's sexual, reproductive and economic freedoms as "prolife," "pro-child" and "pro-family." Media happily adopted the right's manipulative terms of debate, helping to poison public opinion against feminism. *Backlash* exposed the right's linguistic blueprints for political success; if we had taken Faludi's findings seriously then, we might have averted the political morass we're in now. Progressives wondering how we can win back public opinion on our issues should reread *Backlash,* paying special attention to the use of media as political tool.

The Telecommunications Act of 1996, passed under Bill Clinton, compounded this conservative media war by heralding a bigger wave of media mergers than ever before.

Today, a tiny handful of multinationals own the vast majority of newspapers, magazines and network, cable and online news and entertainment outlets, and control not only the reigns of public debate but also record labels, radio stations, theaters, TV and movie production companies, publishing houses, Internet and cable distribution chains, telecom and online companies and advertising billboards...not to mention sports teams, stadiums, theme parks and a myriad of other holdings including investments in the financial services, insurance, medical technology, aircraft engine production, nuclear and weapons manufacturing industries. This presents serious journalistic conflicts of interest: Is it any surprise that news outlets whose parent companies reap hundreds of millions in government subsidies are quick to attack poor mothers' need for food stamps, but slow to critique corporate welfare?

The institutional invisibility of women, people of color, and other public interest voices further skews the news. According to one study by Fairness and Accuracy in Reporting (FAIR), of all U.S. sources interviewed on the national nightly news broadcasts on ABC, NBC and CBS in the entire year of 2001, 92% were white, 85% were male, and, where party affiliation was identifiable, 75 percent were Republican; corporate representatives were regular guests, while public interest voices were absent. As for the powerbrokers behind the scenes, women are just fifteen percent of top executives and twelve percent of board members at Fortune 500 media companies, according to several Annenberg Public Policy Center reports. Worse yet, there are *no woman at all* on the boards of Fox, Clearchannel Radio, Viacom or *The Washington Post*.

We must demand proportional representation. Women are half the population, and we should pressure media to reflect that in their coverage, bylines and in industry leadership.

If more women— and in particular, feminists—were writing, reporting, assigning, analyzing and framing the news, both Bush and Kerry would have been forced, more likely, to campaign on issues such as workplace discrimination, pay equity, reproductive rights, a functional financial safety net, guns, education and more. At the very least, post-election coverage would have focused on the impact of a second Bush term on these and other pressing social issues.

Instead, pundits, op-ed writers, news analysts and reporters responded to the election by telling Democrats to adopt a conservative stance on "moral values," abandon liberal politics and move to the right if they ever want to regain political power.

Contrary to this mantra, we don't need a rightward shift—we need better, broader, more diverse media to ensure the healthy functioning of our democracy. Since structural media reform is key to the potential for future social change, we must urge Senators and Congressmembers to support legislation for diverse, independent and uncensored media. Public interest—not corporate profit—must be the prime motivating factor in media production. Join groups such as Fair.org, the Center for International Media Action (MediaActionCenter.org), FreePress.net, ReclaimTheMedia.org and Media-Alliance.org in the fight to break up the media monopolies, demand open access to the means of production and distribution, and hold corporate media accountable to the public interest. Support organizations such as Women In Media & News (WIMNonline.org), which debunks media bias and trains women's and progressive groups to get their voices heard in public debate, and the Independent Press Association, which amplifies the power of the alternative media.

Building a progressive, feminist media reform movement will take a significant investment of time, energy and resources, but there are also many things we can do individually, everyday. Turn the corporate media monologue into a dialogue: Call, write, and email local, regional and national media outlets, correct the record when our work is misrepresented, expose bias, challenge double standards. Subscribe to independent magazines like *Bitch: Feminist Response to Pop Culture, Extra!* and *In These Times*. Read online independents like CommonDreams.org, WomensEnews.org, LipMagazine.org and AlterNet.org. Watch alternative films from Women Make Movies and Media Education Foundation.

And, if you don't like the media—be the media! Do your own reporting at Indymedia.org, make your own films with PaperTiger.org, and host your own college or community radio show.

The lesson we must take away from the 2004 election is the same one we should have learned from Faludi's *Backlash*: we ignore media at our peril. If we had effectively defended women's rights against conservative media attacks over the last twenty years—and had prioritized structural media reform as a top progressive issue—we could have prevented the slow erosion of an authentic progressive voice in public debate. Now, if we are to reverse the right's rhetorical and legislative victories, we must join together to build a strategic, progressive, feminist media movement to reclaim our media… so that we can take back our country.

OUR MANDATE: MAKING MEDIA MATTER
DANNY SCHECHTER

How can you have any kind of democracy if the people are not informed, not being informed, and in fact being under-informed and uninformed by a system that dumbs it down when we need it to smarten us up?

Network refugee and independent journalist Danny Schechter, "the news dissector," is Executive Editor of Mediachannel.org where his daily blog appears. The former news director of the legendary rock station WBCN-FM in Boston, Schechter was also a producer for CNN and ABC television, and is the author of several books, including *The More You Watch The Less You Know*. His new film *WMD (Weapons of Mass Deception)* takes on the media coverage of the Iraq war.

Knowing that whatever goes up will one day come down or that Nixon fell just months after he was swept back into office no longer reassures.

What seemed clear when the challenger conceded, prematurely many felt, was that even if he had won, the fight would have only begun. He was up against more than one man and his Rove-ing machine, but rather, as the late reggae original Peter Tosh put it, he was fighting the "shit-stem." We all are. As the bombs fell on the Mesopotamian birthplace of world culture, as another election bit the dust, we, many of us anyway, are hell shocked and worse.

Alas, the last place to find out what's really happening is in the places that are supposed to tell us.

And even they admit it.

The Washington Post and *The New York Times* both apologized for their uncritical pro-war coverage. Mea Culpa. And now the network presidents join them. Said ABC's News Chief David Westin the other day: "Simply stated, we let down the American people."

Simply stated, never mind the Iraqi people. They have been put down in the occupation insuring their liberation. This is not simple.

Our ombudsmen now need ombudsmen.

Where did our democracy go? It became a media-ocracy when we weren't looking, with political candidates spending most of their time raising money to buy into a media that often shut them out, as issue-oriented coverage shrunk and the news corps did Bushified their slam dunk. Why are the institutions envisioned and protected as tools for strengthening democracy undermining it?

Another musician, Polarity1, gets it in the way artists can and politician's don't. He asks:

Who owns the media? Who does it speak for?
Your butt on the sofa, leave your mind at the door.
And that's what entertainment is for.
It's the drug of the century, the soul's penitentiary...

And at its heart, and in its entrails, it is our media system that flattens our debates, distorts our perception, corrupts our language, narrows our alternatives, limits our understanding, even as it massages and entertains our brains, reflecting the commercial and political agenda of those on high.

We are one nation under television, swimming/drowning in the digital stream, e-mailing ourselves to death, connecting through cell phones, camera phones, walky-talkies, pagers, PDA's and all the new toys in time for the holiday shopping season that make me yearn for the days when my best buddy and I strung our tin cans between our tenement windows. That was fun and free. Now we have a Verizon on the horizon, more means of communication than of imagination.

We are all talking but are we listening to the drumbeats of homeland insecurity, to the Patriot acts that are anything but? We are yakking away, but what do we have to say?

What is there to say that has not been said?

One set of images flashes in as the others flash out. One minute it is Florida, the next Fallujah—all a non-stop collage that makes everything look and feel like everything else. Oh beautiful for our new digital channels and TIVO machines, for CNN outfoxing Fox and kids glued to news from comedy channels....

We hear but are we heard?

We live through our remote controls without realizing how remote is our own control as we chose between the choices we are given.

It is tempting to spew prose that oozes because it's hard to get a fix on dangerous times, to lock in on our fear of the fear machine. Are we moving back towards the goose-step era or forward beyond the Enron era. Is this progress or regress. How do we know?

We do know that it is not working for us—this military media industrial post-traumatic stress complex driven by a terror war that is not working period. But it is driven by dollops of dollars and has momentum, that big "mo" thing, that is so hard to derail because it not only works on us from outside but more subtly from inside through the constant re-telling of narratives embedded in our mythologies and dream worlds of what we think our country is about.

It helps us think ourselves to sleep

It is this theme of themes that builds the bubbles we live in, that neutralizes unwelcome facts and reinforces those clichés of conformity and cultural understandings that harden partisan attitudes.

It is that theme pounded into us that make us Believers, say amen, in the idea that God, yes God, is blessing America and all will be ok tomorrow when the sun shines and we get up to do it again.

So what do we do now?

The press is supposed to educate
Cast light on the snake, not force-feed the cake
But the state of the press is a crime, it's fake
500 channels—no reason to rejoice
We have too much choice, not enough voice

For one thing, it cannot be one thing. There are too many of us who are angry and estranged, too much to set right, too many levers to pull and changes to be made.

And alas these are not changes we can simply vote for on one morning on one ballot and the birds will sing again. History never happens that way. Just look at our history, from Frederick Douglass who told us "power concedes nothing without a demand" to Martin Luther King who showed we would have to make the change we want to see, to Nelson Mandela and so many heroes who show us it can be done....

Change comes from below, not above, from the outside in, not the inside out. If only our movements would start moving not just "on" but "over" the obstacles in our way, and those obstacles include the idea that a party or a person can be our white knight.

But there are places to begin, to find the path "out of here" as another song once put it....

I am a media maven and so that's where my energy is going. How can you have any kind of democracy if the people are not informed, not being informed, and in fact being under-informed and uninformed by a system that dumbs it down when we need it to smarten us up?

I am convinced we can't fix America without fixing the media system, loosening media concentration, strengthening diversity of perspective, promoting media literacy education, building independent media outlets and challenging the phlegm of mainstream media with some of our own.

Issues are not issues unless and until they are on TV. TV or not to be, that is the question.

I am doing my bit—feeling often like a perpetual motion machine, media channeling, blogging online every morning, dissecting news and offering views, in some rerun of that old speak truth to power routine. By the afternoon, I've shifted into a film-making mode or become a marketing maestro, meeting with activists who are working to lobby more effectively and challenge the templates that keep us locked in place.

My hope is to get everyone I can reach/teach in website range to see that they can get involved in making media matter, in working on media issues where we live and where we think. When will we learn that culture drives politics and not the other way around?

I joined the media thirty years ago to spotlight the problems of the world and discovered the media is one of them, although often unrecognized as such. The last place to look for an understanding of how media works is in the media itself, unless you can decode the code, read between the lines, deconstruct the packaging, and laugh at the ads.

We have purchasing power. Do we use it? We can say no. Do we say it? Do we feedback and talk back? Is our cultural environment just as important to us as our physical environment? Do we act to defend it? You can vote with your eyeballs and with your ears as well as your ballot. We can demand more than we are getting from our media that thrives on free access to airwaves that belong to all of us.

To find out what they don't tell you, visit specialized web sites like the Media Alliance (media-alliance.org) or our Mediachannel.org, a super-site featuring journalism from hundreds of news organizations worldwide. Enroll in our Media for Democracy network (a "MoveOn.org" on the media, organizing actions on media related issues) to add your input to the fight for a better output.

Can we put the "public" back in public broadcasting with more than just our pledge dollars, which are taken for granted anyway? Neo-con leaning political appointees to the Corporation for Public Broadcasting, the agency established by Congress to shield public broadcasting from political pressure, have gained power and are now affecting programming.

Can we take a stand on these issues, like those three million Americans who flooded the FCC with letters protesting the relaxing of ownership rules that allowed for more moguls to merge? That grassroots outpouring shocked the media, and with the help of the courts, slowed down the process toward even greater consolidation.

Do you know that we are not alone? Few surveys survey our attitudes towards media but when they do they report a consensus of complaint. Seventy percent dissatisfaction with those who are "only giving us what we want."

Seventy percent for different reasons of course, but what else can seventy percent of Americans agree on? And by-the-by, when the same questions are put to people in the media, seventy percent of them agree the system is dysfunctional, doing far more harm than good.

"Simply stated," there is hope.

I read the news about the news today. Oh boy.

Lyric of "News Goo (The More You Watch the Less You Know)" ©1997 Polar Levine

THE
SEPARATION
OF CHURCH
AND STATE

LESSONS FROM THE CHRISTIAN RIGHT
ESTHER KAPLAN

We can never confront our current political dilemma effectively if we deny that the Christian right is a potent political force that turned out millions to vote for George W. Bush precisely because they support holy war, they want a Christian government, and they see in the President an ally in their struggle to restore a traditional social order in which homosexuality is a sin and women don't control their own reproductive lives.

Esther Kaplan is a radio and print journalist; a frequent contributor to *The Nation*; a contributing editor at *Poz*, the national AIDS magazine; and the author of *With God on Their Side: How Christian Fundamentalists Trampled Science, Policy, and Democracy in George W. Bush's White House.*

In 1989, with illness everywhere and no effective AIDS treatments in sight, cultural critic Douglas Crimp wrote a landmark essay about the AIDS movement he called "Mourning and Militancy." Watching the activists around him face burnout and emotional exhaustion as they spent afternoons at the hospital, evenings in the meeting hall, and weekends at funerals, he argued that we have to mourn *and* organize. That it's simply too hard to move forward if we suppress our grief.[1]

We have to mourn now, too. And by that I mean we have to loosen our stiff upper lips and acknowledge the terrible fix we're in. After a frenzy of door-knocking and phone-banking and a record turnout at the polls, a majority of American voters reelected a man who sanctions torture, wages preemptive war, and profits from hatred toward Muslims and gays. They chose someone determined to make the rich richer and the poor poorer, a son of privilege who has surrounded himself with people who believe his presidency was ordained by God. Not only did he win reelection, but George W. Bush's party gained seats in Congress and he is poised to remake the Supreme Court. The majority of governorships and state legislatures are also now in Republican hands, as is most of the federal bench. Even worse, riding on the surge in the "moral values" vote, leaders of the Christian right are claiming full credit for this total victory and have declared, "Now comes the revolution."[2] We have lost, and we have lost terribly. It's time for a reckoning.

We can and should demand full recounts of the vote, and raise questions about the way exit pollers frame questions about morality. But we can never confront our current political dilemma effectively if we deny that the Christian right is a potent political force that turned out millions of the faithful to vote for George W. Bush precisely because they support holy war, they want a Christian government, and they see in the President an ally in their struggle to restore a traditional social order in which homosexuality is a sin and women don't control their own reproductive lives. As a voting bloc, they are impressively immune to inspectors who prove there were no WMDs in Iraq, or officials who announce that job numbers are down, because they are attached to the president, umbilically, as a brother in faith. This loyalty is mutual, of course, as Bush spent much of his first term opening up our federal coffers, and the halls of power, to this most cherished of his constituencies.

An irony of history is that this rise to power by the Christian right was sparked by a moment of defeat as absolute for the right as this one was for the left. The resounding defeat of presidential candidate Barry Goldwater in 1964, the gains made by the civil rights movement, and the rise of the late '60s counterculture set off deep soul-searching among conservatives, who were forced to realize that they'd lost the battle for the hearts and minds of America. So they set about to rebuild, almost from scratch, a new coalition that would have the potential to retake power. A key element in this game plan was the development of a new Southern strategy based on social values. Richard Viguerie, Paul Weyrich, and other right-wing strategists targeted the once liberal evangelical movement—which had been in retreat from political life for decades—and willed the Christian right into being, carving out mobilize-able constituencies, issue by issue, through direct mail operations, and tapping the Reverend Jerry Falwell to start up the movement's founding organization, the Moral Majority. Slowly, from clusters of followers surrounding a handful of charismatic leaders, the movement built institutional power. Think tanks, such as the Heritage Foundation; issue-based lobbies, such as the National Right to Life Committee; and conservative Christian media empires such as Focus on the Family cropped up throughout the 1970s. In 1980, the movement helped push Reagan into office; ten years later the Christian Coalition arrived on the scene with its national network and powerful ability to mobilize the grass roots. Now the movement has hundreds of national and local membership organizations, many with $100 million budgets, as well as thousands of radio and television outfits reaching tens of millions of listeners, several well-funded think tanks and political action committees, professional associations and journals, deep-pocketed funders dedicated to long-term institution-building, and a massive network of tens of thousands of churches and ministries. Christian right leaders commandeered entire denominations, such as the

Southern Baptist Convention, by purging theological moderates, and they invaded the Republican Party as well.[3] A 2002 analysis in the trade journal *Campaigns and Elections* found that in 44 states, Christian conservatives have a decisive influence on Republican state committees, up from 31 just six years earlier. The movement has a fertile farm system, too, which attracts young people through youth ministries and cultivates new political leaders by running Christian right activists as candidates for school boards and city councils. Now, scattered in key positions within the White House, Justice, State, and Health and Human Services, they're running the federal government.

And they certainly didn't come this far by triangulating their politics or by sublimating their core concerns for the greater good of the Republican Party. They did it by staking out inflexible positions and then building a political constituency around them over the course of decades. Christian right leaders have often threatened, petulantly, to keep their followers away from the polls. Or they've refused to endorse Republican Party presidential candidates, bolting for the insurgencies of Pat Robertson and Howard Phillips rather than compromise on their ideals. They have helped defeat Republican presidential bids, such as George Bush Sr.'s reelection campaign, during which Pat Buchanan alienated swing voters by shouting about culture war from the stage of the Republican National Convention. They have clung to unpopular positions, such as outlawing abortion and funding abstinence-only education, in the face of a solid pro-choice majority and the desire by at least 75 percent of American parents to have their children get sex ed that covers birth control and condoms. Republican victory, per se, was never their goal. They only fell in line behind the GOP leadership in 2000 and 2004, agreeing to stay out of the convention spotlight, because they trusted so deeply that they were helping to elect a kindred spirit.

Thomas Frank, the author of *What's the Matter with Kansas*, has claimed that red staters were duped into voting against their class interests by a values agenda that politicians never really deliver on, anyway. But these values voters have hardly gone home empty-handed, as Frank supposes. Bush has defunded Christian right public enemies such as Planned Parenthood and the UN Population Fund and signed a "partial birth abortion" ban, the first federal legislation to restrict abortion access since *Roe v. Wade*. He has granted tens of millions of dollars in federal faith-based pork to pro-life "crisis pregnancy centers" and charities run by the likes of Pat Robertson and Chuck Colson and enshrined embryonic personhood in federal law. He has censored information on condoms and he has appointed federal judges who support prayer in our public schools. The president has delivered for the Christian right so handsomely that not long ago Gary Bauer declared him the new leader of the movement. Many voting blocs— Jews, for example—vote against their narrow class interest in order to defend their cultural values. That's what "moral values" voters did in November, with their eyes wide open.

If there's a lesson to be learned from the Christian right's ascendancy, it's not that liberals and progressives should blur their identities by tacking to the center or join in the anti-gay chorus, as Bill Clinton has shamefully suggested. It's that those of us on the radical fringe of the Democratic Party, including some of the millions of Americans who are too skeptical or disenchanted to vote at all, should strongly assert our own values agenda and dig in for a decade or two to build a formidable political force, one that could yank the Democrats back to the left and fuel a progressive resurgence.

What might such a strategy look like? It will have to involve activating the religious left. The potential is there, judging by recent positions embraced, to little fanfare, by the U.S. Catholic Bishops, liberal evangelicals, and the mainline Protestants of the National Council of Churches against unjust wars and policies that punish the poor. It would mean building up a progressive media network to rival the far right's. The recent spike in sales of books from left presses such as South End and the New Press, in subscriptions to *The Nation*, and in syndication of radio programs such as Air America and Democracy Now provide momentum for such an effort. Recall that in 1979, the Christian right didn't have much more than Jerry Falwell's weekly broadcasts from Thomas Road

Baptist Church. It would mean activating new voters around issues that spark passion, such as criminal justice reform for African Americans, and immigration law liberalization for Asians and Latinos. It would mean pulling some socially conservative, white working class Catholics and Protestants back into the fold through a strong program for economic justice. The AFL-CIO has already shown that this can be done: while 22 percent of voters listed "moral values" as their top priority, only 16 percent of union families did, and their heightened concern over issues such as health care access, overtime pay, and the minimum wage delivered a majority of white union voters to the Democrats—even though whites as a whole went for Bush. It would mean putting our own true believers into Congress and defending them when they introduce, and fight like hell for, ambitious legislation. It would mean believing in our own values and trying to win power for their sake, not in the service of some shell of a Democratic Party that hates gays a little less and puts a sunnier face on U.S. empire.

So let's mourn this loss. And once it hits us that we've got nothing left to lose, let's get more militant.

---

[1] Douglas Crimp, "Mourning and Militancy," *October* 51 (Winter 1989). It was filmmaker and AIDS activist Gregg Bordowitz who first pointed out the relevance of Crimp's old essay for the current moment, in a late November talk at Cooper Union in New York City.

[2] Richard Viguerie, the direct mail guru of the far right, quoted in David D. Kirkpatrick, "Some Supporters Say They Anticipate a 'Revolution,'" *New York Times*, November 4, 2004.

[3] Excellent sources on this history are Sara Diamond, *Roads to Dominion: Right-Wing Movements and Political Power in America* (Guilford, 1995) and Jean Hardisty, *Mobilizing Resentment: Conservative Resurgence from the John Birch Society to the Promise Keepers* (Beacon, 1999).

REPUBLICANS BANK ON BLACK EVANGELICALS TO HELP THEM KEEP WINNING

EARL OFARI HUTCHINSON

If they are to have any hope of stopping their current presidential and congressional political hemorrhaging, top Democrats must short-circuit the evangelical push for black votes.

Earl Ofari Hutchinson is an author and political analyst. He is the author of *The Crisis in Black and Black*. He is the publisher of The Hutchinson Report Newsletter, an on-line public issues newsletter.

In post-election exit polls, a majority of black evangelicals said that jobs, the economy, health care, and education topped their list of concerns. In the volumes of election post-mortems, black leaders and top Democrats seized on that as proof that though Bush got a marginal bump up in black support, Republicans failed miserably to get blacks to break Democratic ranks and vote en masse for him.

They're right and wrong. Republicans spent millions on ads on black radio stations, successfully wooed a handful of high profile black preachers, and touted the supposed glories of Bush's faith based initiative. Yet, Bush got at best only a two to three percent rise nationally in black support over what he got in 2000. But that doesn't mean the money, time and effort of Republicans was a waste. If anything, it turned out to be the best bargain of the campaign for them.

The great election paradox was that while black evangelicals voted overwhelmingly for John Kerry, they also gave Bush the cushion he needed to bag Ohio and the White House. There were early warning signs that this might happen. The same polls that showed black's prime concern was with bread and butter issues and that Kerry was the guy that could deliver the most for them, also showed that a sizeable number of blacks ranked abortion, gay marriage, and school prayer as priority issues for them. Their concern for these issues didn't come anywhere close to that of white evangelicals. However, it was still higher than the concern the general voting public had for these issues.

A Joint Center for Political and Economic Studies poll in 2004 found that blacks by a far bigger margin than the overall population opposed gay marriage.

The reasons for this anti-gay bias are easy to find. From cradle to grave, many black men have believed and accepted the gender propaganda that real men talk and act tough, shed no tears, and never show their emotions. When black men broke the prescribed male code of conduct and showed their feelings they were harangued as weaklings, and their manhood instantly questioned. In a vain attempt to recapture their denied masculinity, many black men mirrored America's traditional fear and hatred of homosexuality as a dire threat to their manhood.

Many blacks, in an attempt to distance themselves from gays and avoid confronting their own fears and biases, dismissed homosexuality as a perverse contrivance of white males that reflected the decadence of white America. While many Americans made gays their gender bogeymen, many blacks made gay men their bogeymen and waged open warfare against them. Many black ministers, as many white Christian fundamentalist ministers, wave the Bible and rail against homosexuality as the defiler of faith and family values.

A survey that measured black attitudes toward gays published in *Jet Magazine* in 1994 found that a sizable number of blacks were suspicious and scornful of gays. The poll would probably find attitudes among blacks have not changed much since then.

Many blacks also loathed Kerry's perceived support of abortion, and gay rights. In polls, he got twenty percent less support from black conservative evangelicals than Democratic presidential contender Al Gore got in 2000. In the right place and under the right circumstance, black evangelicals could pose a stealth danger to Kerry. As it turned out, the right place for Bush was Ohio, and the right circumstance was the state's gay marriage ban initiative, and a band of activist and outspoken black evangelical leaders that backed the ban and Bush.

The sixteen percent of Ohio blacks, or about 90,000 voters, that voted for Bush was significantly higher than the overall black vote total nationally. It proved crucial to his victory on two counts. If Kerry had nabbed these votes he would have been in striking distance of winning Ohio outright. Even if he didn't, they would have considerably shaved down Bush's relatively slender vote margin over Kerry. He and top Democrats would have thought much harder about conceding the election as fast as they did to Bush. The vote closeness would have justified a demand that the election not be certified until the more than 200,000 provisional and absentee ballots were counted. That would have taken days, but it would have kept Democrats hopes alive that they could still snatch victory from what appeared to be defeat. It didn't happen and it will be chalked up as yet another tantalizing what if of presidential elections.

But there's no "what if" about the black evangelicals. The helpful nudge over the top that they gave Bush in Ohio was not lost on Bush's political architect Karl Rove and conservative pro-family groups. They have publicly declared that they will pour even more resources, time and attention into revving up black evangelicals in the 2006 and 2008 national and presidential elections. Rove has flatly said that Bush will try to pay off one of his debts to evangelicals by pushing the languishing federal gay marriage ban. Family groups say they'll dump gay marriage ban initiatives on ballots in as many states as they can. In some of those states, such as Michigan, where blacks make up a significant percent of voters, and they backed that state's gay marriage ban in big numbers, Republicans will inflame blacks' anti-gay bias.

Even if passage of the federal marriage ban ultimately falls flat on its face if it gets out of Congress to the states, the fight over it can still turn the 2006 mid-term and 2008 presidential elections into a noisy and distracting referendum on the family. That will give Republican strategists another chance to pose as God's defenders of the family and shove even more black evangelicals into the Republican vote column.

In the flush of their Bush victory, evangelical leaders and conservative pro-family groups boast that the issues of war and peace, and jobs and the economy will take a back seat to moral values in future elections. If they're right, they'll get a hearing from even more black evangelicals. That's no guarantee that their votes again will help tip the White House to Republicans. But it could spell more peril in future elections for the Democrats.

If they are to have any hope of stopping their current presidential and congressional political hemorrhaging, top Democrats must short-circuit the evangelical push for black votes. That means not abandoning their tradition and vision of being the party that stands for peace, prosperity, economic security, and equally important, civil rights, civil liberties and social justice. After all, the majority of African-Americans still voted for and will continue to vote for Democrats, and that includes many black evangelicals whom, as the polls showed, still considered economic and social justice issues critically important.

By being true to their proud traditions, the Democrats can eventually seize back the political high ground. When they do, the overwhelming majority of African-Americans will stand on that high ground with them.

FIGHTING WORDS FOR A SECULAR AMERICA
ROBIN MORGAN

When George W. Bush and his Cabinet members invoke the "Christian Fathers of our country," the Founders must be picketing in their graves.

A founder of contemporary U.S. feminism, Robin Morgan has been a leader in the international women's movement for 25 years, as well as an award-winning writer, political theorist, poet, journalist, and editor. She has published 18 books, including three classic anthologies: *Sisterhood Is Powerful*; *Sisterhood Is Global*; and *Sisterhood Is Forever: The Women's Anthology for A New Millennium*. Her newest books include *Saturday's Child: A Memoir*; and her best-selling *The Demon Lover: The Roots of Terrorism*.

Americans who honor the U.S. Constitution's separation of church and state are alarmed. Agnostic and atheists, as well as observant people of every faith, fear the religious right has gained historic political power via an ultraconservative movement with highly placed friends. But many of us feel helpless. We haven't read the Founding Documents since school (if then). We lack arguing tools, "verbal karate" evidence we can cite to defend a secular United States.

For instance, extremists claim—and, too-often, we ourselves assume—that U.S. law has religious roots. Yet the Constitution contains no reference to a deity. The Declaration of Independence contains not one word on religion, basing its authority on the shocking idea that power is derived from ordinary people, which challenged European traditions of rule by divine right and/or heavenly authority. (Remember, George III was king of England *and* anointed head of its church.) The words "Nature's God," the "Creator," and "Divine Providence" do appear in the Declaration. But in its context—an era and author, Thomas Jefferson—that celebrated science and The Enlightenment, these words are analogous to our contemporary phrase, "life force."

Rev. Jerry Falwell notoriously blamed 9/11 on "pagans, abortionists, feminists, gays and lesbians… groups who have tried to secularize America." He's a bit late. In 1798, Alexander Hamilton accused Jefferson of a "conspiracy to establish atheism on the ruins of Christianity" in the new republic.

Undersecretary of Defense William Boykin thunders, "We're a Christian nation." But the 1796 Treaty of Tripoli—initiated by George Washington and signed into law by John Adams—proclaims: *"The government of the United States of America is not in any sense founded on the Christian Religion."*

Offices for "Faith-Based Initiatives" with nearly $20 billion in grants have been established (by executive order, circumventing Congress) in ten federal agencies, as well as *inside* the White House. This violates "the Lemon Test," a 1971 Supreme Court decision (*Lemon v. Kurtzman*): "(i) a statute [or public policy] must have a secular legislative purpose; (ii) the principal effect of the statute [or policy] must neither advance nor inhibit religion; (iii) the statute [or policy] must not foster 'excessive [government] entanglement with religion.'"

"Traditionalists" rabid to keep inserting "under God" in the Pledge of Allegiance are actually *anti*-tradition. Those words never appeared in the original, penned in 1892 by Rev. Francis Bellamy (a Baptist forced to resign the pulpit for having called himself a Christian socialist). After intense lobbying by the Knights of Columbus and American Legion, "One nation, indivisible" was changed by Congress to "One nation *under God*, indivisible"; this was in 1954, reflecting McCarthyite bombast against "godless Communism" at the Cold War's height. (Francis Bellamy's granddaughter, Barbara Bellamy Wright, denounced the revision, noting her grandfather "would have objected strongly.") On Flag Day, 1943, the Supreme Court (*West Virginia State Board of Education v. Barnette*) ruled unconstitutional a law compelling schoolchildren to recite the pledge and salute the flag. For the Court, Justice Jackson wrote, "If there is any fixed star in our constitutional constellation, it is that no official, high or petty, can prescribe what shall be orthodox in politics, nationalism, religion, or other matters of opinion."

What about our currency? Originally, the motto on coins (the major exchange medium in the 18th century) was simply: "Liberty." But "In God We Trust" began to appear informally on some U.S. coins during the 19th century, due to a spread of religious fervor following the Civil War. Yet early in the 20th century, when President Theodore Roosevelt commissioned the design for new coinage, he left *off* "In God We Trust," expressing his "very firm conviction that to put such a motto on coins . . . not only does no good but does positive harm." Congress overrode him in 1908, after a lengthy crusade initiated by a hyper-religious director of the Mint, James Pollock. A campaign of petitions from religious congregations so frightened Rough Rider Roosevelt that he conceded, announcing he wouldn't veto the bill. Paper currency escaped deification until 1957: religious advocates began agitating for the words during the 1940s—but not until those McCarthyite 1950s did they succeed. The Fifties also saw IGWT's adoption as the national "motto." The Founders would be outraged. Their original motto and Great Seal—devised by Adams, Franklin, and Jefferson—was "E Pluribus Unum" ("From Many, One"), which, with "Liberty," was considered appropriate and sufficient, until the charge of the god brigades.

Furthermore, the only oath of office specified verbatim in The Constitution (Article II, Section 1) is that taken by the President, and *the words "so help me God" do not appear in it.* On the contrary, the Founders deliberately noted the vow could be sworn as an oath or simply *affirmed.* Listing the secular choice of "affirmation" as the coequal alternative to a religious "oath" is in itself remarkably radical for its time

The Constitution itself *contains not one reference to a deity or any supernatural powers.* This is not an oversight. In fact, the word "religious" occurs only once, in Article VI: "Senators and Representatives . . . shall be bound by oath or affirmation, to support this Constitution; *but no religious test shall ever be required as a qualification to any office or public trust under the United States."*

When George W. Bush and his Cabinet members invoke the "Christian Fathers of our country," the Founders must be picketing in their graves. They were a mix of freethinkers, atheists, Christians, agnostics, Freemasons, and Deists (professing belief in powers scientifically evinced in the natural universe). They were definitely imperfect. Some were slaveholders. Female citizens were invisible to them—though Abigail Adams warned her husband John, "If particular care and attention are not paid to the ladies, we are determined to foment a rebellion and will not hold ourselves bound to obey any laws in which we have no voice or representation."

But the Founders were, after all, *revolutionaries.* Their passion—especially regarding secularism—glows through their documents and personal correspondence.

Thomas Paine

Paine's writings heavily influenced the other Founders. A freethinker who opposed all organized religion, he reserved particular vituperation for Christianity.

"My country is the world and my religion is to do good" (*The Rights of Man*, 1791).

"I do not believe in the creed professed by the Jewish church, by the Roman church, by the Greek church, by the Protestant church, nor by any church that I know of. My own mind is my church" (*The Age of Reason*, 1793).

"Of all the systems of religion that ever were invented, there is no more derogatory to the Almighty, more unedifying to man, more repugnant to reason, and more contradictory to itself than this thing called Christianity" (*Ibid.*)

Benjamin Franklin

Raised a Calvinist, Franklin rebelled—and spread that rebellion, affecting Adams and Jefferson. His friend, Dr. Priestley, wrote in his own *Autobiography*: "It is much to be lamented that a man of Franklin's general good character and great influence should have been an unbeliever in Christianity, and also have done as much as he did to make others unbelievers." A scientist, Franklin rejected churches, rituals, and all "supernatural superstitions."

"Scarcely was I arrived at fifteen years of age, when, after having doubted in turn of different tenets, according as I found them combated in the different books that I read, I began to doubt of Revelation itself" (Franklin's *Autobiography*, *1731-1759*).

"Some books against Deism fell into my hands . . . they wrought an effect on me quite contrary to what was intended by them; for the arguments of the Deists, which were quoted to be refuted, appeared to me much stronger than the refutations; in short, I soon became a thorough Deist" (*Ibid.*).

George Washington

The false image of Washington as a devout Christian was fabricated by Mason Locke Weems, a clergyman who also invented the cherry-tree fable and in 1800 published his *Life of George Washington*. Washington, a

Deist and a Freemason, never once mentioned the name of Jesus Christ in any of his thousands of letters, and pointedly referred to divinity as "It." Whenever he (rarely) attended church, Washington always deliberately left before communion, demonstrating disbelief in Christianity's central ceremony.

John Adams

Adams, a Unitarian inspired by The Enlightenment, fiercely opposed doctrines of supernaturalism or damnation, writing to Jefferson: "I almost shudder at the thought of alluding to the most fatal example of the abuses of grief which the history of mankind has preserved—the Cross. Consider what calamities that engine of grief has produced!"

Adams realized how politically crucial—and imperiled—a secular state would be:

"The United States of America have exhibited, perhaps, the first example of governments erected on the simple principles of nature; and if men are now sufficiently enlightened to disabuse themselves of artifice, imposture, hypocrisy, and superstition, they will consider this event as an era in their history. . . . It will never be pretended that any persons employed in that service [forming the U.S. government] had interviews with the gods, or were in any degree under the influence of heaven, more than those at work upon ships or houses, or laboring in merchandise or agriculture; it will forever be acknowledged that these governments were contrived merely by the use of reason and the senses. . . . Thirteen governments [the original states] thus founded on the natural authority of the people alone, without a pretence of miracle or mystery... are a great point gained in favor of the rights of mankind" (*A Defense of the Constitutions of Government of the United States of America,* 1787-1788).

Thomas Jefferson

It's a commonly stated error that U.S. law, based on English common law, is thus grounded in Judeo-Christian tradition. Yet Jefferson (writing to Thomas Cooper, February 10, 1814) noted that common law "is that system of law introduced by the Saxons on their settlement in England . . . about the middle of the fifth century. But Christianity was not introduced till the seventh century. . . . *We may safely affirm (though contradicted by all the judges and writers on earth) that Christianity neither is, nor ever was, a part of the common law.*"

Jefferson professed disbelief in the Trinity and the divinity of Jesus Christ, while respecting moral teachings by whomever might have been an historical Jesus. He cut up a Bible, assembling his own version: "The whole history of these books [the Gospels] is so defective and doubtful. . ." he wrote Adams (January 24, 1814), "evidence that parts have proceeded from an extraordinary man; and that other parts are of the fabric of very inferior minds."

Scorning miracles, saints, salvation, damnation, and angelic presences, Jefferson embraced reason, materialism, and science. He challenged Patrick Henry, who wanted a Christian theocracy:

". . . an amendment was proposed by inserting "Jesus Christ," so that [the preamble] would read 'A departure from the plan of Jesus Christ, the holy author of our religion;' the insertion was rejected by the great majority, in proof that they meant to comprehend, within the mantle of its protection, the Jew and the Gentile, the Christian and Mohammedan, the Hindoo and Infidel of every denomination" (from Jefferson's *Autobiography*, referring to the Virginia Act for Religious Freedom).

The theme is consistent throughout Jefferson's prolific correspondence:

"Question with boldness even the existence of a god" (letter to Peter Carr, August 10, 1787).

"I contemplate with sovereign reverence that act of the whole American people which [built] a wall of separation between church and State" (letter to the Danbury [Connecticut] Baptist Association, January 1, 1802).

"History, I believe, furnishes no example of a priest-ridden people maintaining a free civil government" (letter to Alexander von Humboldt, December 6, 1813).

"In every country and in every age, the priest has been hostile to liberty. He is always in alliance with the despot, abetting his abuses in return for protection to his own" (letter to Horatio G. Spafford, March 17, 1814).

"Whence arises the morality of the Atheist?... Their virtue, then, must have had some other foundation than the love of God" (letter to Thomas Law, June 13, 1814).

"I am of a sect by myself, as far as I know" (letter to Ezra Stiles Ely, June 25, 1819).

"The day will come when the mystical generation of Jesus . . . will be classed with the fable of the generation of Minerva in the brain of Jupiter" (letter to John Adams, April 11, 1823).

James Madison

Although prayer groups proliferate in today's Congress, James Madison, "father of the Constitution," denounced even the presence of *chaplains* in Congress—*and* in the armed forces—as unconstitutional. He opposed all use of "religion as an engine of civil policy," and accurately prophesied the threat of "ecclesiastical corporations."

"Religious bondage shackles and debilitates the mind and unfits it for every noble enterprise" (letter to William Bradford, April 1, 1774).

"What influence, in fact, have ecclesiastical establishments had on society? In some instances they have been seen to erect a spiritual tyranny on the ruins of the civil authority; in many instances they have been seen upholding the thrones of political tyranny; in no instance have they been the guardians of the liberties of the people. Rulers who wish to subvert the public liberty may have found an established clergy convenient auxiliaries" (*Memorial and Remonstrance against Religious Assessments*, Section 8, 1785).

"Besides the danger of a direct mixture of Religion & Civil Government, there is an evil which ought to be guarded against in the indefinite accumulation of property from the capacity of holding it in perpetuity by ecclesiastical corporations. The power of all corporations ought to be limited in this respect.... The establishment of the chaplainship to Congress is a palpable violation of equal rights, as well as of Constitutional principles.... Better also to disarm, in the same way, the precedent of chaplainships for the army and navy. . . . Religious proclamations by the Executive [branch] recommending thanksgivings & fasts are shoots from the same root.... Altho' recommendations only, they imply a religious agency, making no part of the trust delegated to political rulers" (*"Monopolies, Perpetuities, Corporations, Ecclesiastical Endowments,"* ca. 1817).

That's only a sampling: quotes that blast cobwebs off our tamed images of the Founders. Their own statements—not dead rhetoric but alive with ringing, still radical, ideas—can reconnect us to our proud, secular roots, and inspire us to defend them. Activist sources for doing so include: Americans United for Separation of Church and State (*www.au.org*), Freedom from Religion Foundation (*www.ffrf.org*), and People for the American Way (*www.pfaw.org*).

In these times of bitterly contentious non-dialogue, progressive people of faith in particular can do much-needed, vital work in their own communities, e.g. Texas Faith Network (*www.tfn.org*). For women this fight is especially crucial: we're "canaries in the mine," the first to suffer from escalating religious-based restrictions attacking our right to reproductive choice; to government-funded shelters and programs for survivors of rape, domestic violence, and child abuse; to affirmative action; to equal-opportunity access to education and jobs; to redefining "family" as more inclusive, and more. *Feminist.com* is an excellent website to find and hyperlink with a wide array of groups focusing on different priority issues.

But this work needs *all* of us—men, women, *and* children, red- *and* blue-staters. Whatever our beliefs, we all need to acknowledge this grave threat to our secular, pluralistic society—a threat that at its worst openly declares its goal of an American Christian theocracy, and at its least inflicts severely chilling effects on freedoms the Founders defined. We need to stand up to *all* forms of bigotry (even when disguised as biblical). We need to get on local school boards and city councils, to protect our rights to read fine literature and teach sound science. We need to educate ourselves and each other, to quote the Founders' words in letters to newspaper editors, in calls to local TV and talk-radio, in pressuring our Congressional Representatives and Senators.

The Founders minced no words—and they acted on them.

Dare we do less?

THE
ENVIRONMENT

THE OBLIGATION TO ENDURE... AGAIN....
SANDRA STEINGRABER

Between the overwhelming and the trivial lies another path.

Sandra Steingraber, Ph.D., is a visiting scholar at Ithaca College in New York. The recipient of the Rachel Carson Leadership Award in 2001, she is the author of *Living Downstream: An Ecologist Looks at Cancer and the Environment* and *Having Faith: An Ecologist's Journey to Motherhood.*

For many years public-spirited citizens throughout the country have been working for the conservation of the natural resources, realizing their vital importance to the Nation. Apparently, their hard-won progress is to be wiped out, as a politically minded Administration returns us to the dark ages of unrestrained exploitation and destruction. It is one of the ironies of our time that while concentrating on the defense of our country against enemies from without, we should be so heedless of those who would destroy it from within.

These bitter words appeared in a letter to the editor of the *Washington Post* in April, 1953. The Republicans had just won the White House. Joseph McCarthy held ruthless sway in the Senate. The long-time director of the Fish and Wildlife Service had just been dismissed.

The author of this letter was a young biologist named Rachel Carson.

Carson could not have known, when she penned it, how profound an impact her short letter would have. The Associated Press picked it up for syndication. The *Reader's Digest* reprinted it. And so her missive found its way onto front porches and breakfast tables, into living rooms and libraries and doctors' office waiting rooms across the nation. At the height of the Cold War, in the midst of an anti-Communist inquisition that had convulsed the federal government, Carson's assertion that "the real wealth of the Nation lies in the resources of the earth—soil, water, forests, minerals, and wildlife" struck a chord with the populace. In this way, she opened up a critical space in the paranoid culture of her time to have a conversation about the environment.

But Carson could not have foreseen all this when she pulled the pages of her letter from the typewriter, folded them into the envelope, and rummaged through her desk for a postage stamp. Nor could she have guessed the effect that the letter's publication would ultimately have on her own life as writer. In 1953, Carson was the author of gentle, lyrical books about the sea. Now she spoke as a blistering critic. And when, nine years later, she combined her political voice with the poetry of her descriptive nature writing, the result was her masterpiece, *Silent Spring*, which, broadly speaking, argued that the contamination of our environment with inherently poisonous chemicals is a basic violation of human rights. The publication of this book in 1962 did more to galvanize the environmental movement than any other single event. *Silent Spring* gave us the Environmental Protection Agency and inspired almost every major piece of environmental legislation on the books.

So, as I read the letter written to a newspaper editor 52 years ago while listening to John Kerry concede the election with votes still uncounted in Ohio, I found the following reasons for hope . . . .

First, we are not the only generation of thoughtful people with an abiding appreciation for groundwater, oxygen, and birdsong to ever be ruled over by men utterly unconcerned with the ongoing destruction of ecological systems—and who indeed may be directly profiting by it. It is comforting to feel the presence of those reformers who came before us, to know ourselves as their heirs. Carson herself pays homage in *Silent Spring* to one of her own heroes, the French biologist Jean Rostand, who said, "the obligation to endure gives us the right to know."

Second, we owe it to these forebears—who sometimes labored at great personal cost to their health and reputation—to overcome our collective despair and figure out how best to carry on. Consider that Carson composed many of *Silent Spring's* sentences after 11:30 PM when she finally got her household settled. She was a single mother, the sole caretaker of an aged parent, and a breast cancer patient. She took on the pesticide industry and the U.S. Department of Agriculture while on chemotherapy. Her editor was threatened with lawsuits.

Third, out of a dark period of history can sometimes emerge a redeeming idea that lights the way for years to come.

And, fourth, such an illuminating idea may not arrive full-blown on the scene. It may begin in small ways and with other intents and purposes. As when someone objects in the newspaper to the firing of a fine public servant.[1]

As a biologist and author myself, I labor in the fields that Carson planted. I don't have any single answer to the question of what we do about the next four years, but I do have a few observations to offer from seven years of travel with my own two books. These come from conversations I've had in the hallways of the European Union's Parliament, as well as those conducted in church basements in eastern Montana and in assorted conference halls, libraries, barns, and community centers where I have been kindly invited. They come from comments made by farmers, architects, pediatricians, firefighters, chefs, auto workers, fashion designers, college students, cancer survivors, radio talk show hosts, athletes, and filmmakers.

Letters to the editor are good. They are still among the most widely read features of the daily paper. A simple, 200-word letter expressing concern about a local environmental issue has served as a powerful organizing tool in many communities. If you are at a loss for what to write about, explore the Toxics Release Inventory for your hometown zip code (www.rtknet.org or www.scorecard.org). This is the federal database of information about toxic chemical releases, mandated by the hard-won Emergency Planning and Community Right-to-Know Act that passed Congress by one vote in 1986. It is the pollution disclosure program that Carson called for in *Silent Spring* and that was imagined before her by Jean Rostand.

Right-to-know is currently under fresh assault by those who prefer secrecy about toxic chemicals to public revelation and who are now couching their arguments in the language of homeland security. (If we stop disclosing the location of poisonous chemicals in our communities, the terrorists will not find them.) Real homeland security necessitates chemical security, not chemical ignorance. (For more on this battle, get in touch with the Working Group on Community Right-to-Know or the government watchdog group OMB Watch.) And meaningful chemical security includes substituting safer materials for explosive, poisonous ones that could easily be turned into weapons of mass destruction. (For more on this, get in touch with Greenpeace.)

Inspiration can be found abroad. It is easy in the United States— with its mythos of can-do ingenuity—to think that if our nation is not leading the charge, there is no charge. But consider the Stockholm Convention, a United Nations treaty that aims to rid the world of persistent organic pollutants. These are a dangerous class of chemicals that travel globally, are highly toxic to people and wildlife, and siphon their way up the food chain. No nation can manage them alone. Dioxin is one example. The pesticide DDT is another. So far, the Stockholm Convention has been signed by 89 nation states, and it bans or otherwise heavily restricts the use of twelve such chemicals. The United States has not ratified the treaty and fought hard to weaken it. On May 14, 2004, the Stockholm Convention became international law anyway.

Or consider REACH, the revolutionary new policy proposal for the regulation of chemicals within the European Union. The seeds of REACH were planted in 1998 when the governments of the EU member states renounced the previous policy as "unable to protect people and the environment in a satisfactory way against negative effects." The original proposal, therefore, placed the burden of proof for safety squarely on industry by requiring adequate scientific data as a pre-condition for marketing chemicals. It also included a mechanism for replacing hazardous materials with safer ones. At this writing, REACH is still a work in progress. The International Chemical Secretariat in Sweden serves as a citizen watchdog for the legislative process.

Or consider Canadian grass. Nearly 70 municipalities in Canada now prohibit the use of pesticides for cosmetic reasons, that is, to improve the appearance of lawns and gardens. These include the city of Toronto as well as the entire province of Quebec. These bans have been upheld by the Canadian Supreme Court and are supported by the Canadian Cancer Society, which describes the evidence linking lawn chemicals and certain cancers as suggestive enough to warrant precautionary action: "When an activity raises threats of harm to human health or to the environment, precautionary measures should be taken, even if some cause-and-effect relationships are not fully established scientifically."

So perhaps we don't need to move to Canada—just replicate their toxic-free lawns, parks, and gardens here. (To learn how, read "Canadian Activists Win Pesticide Bylaws," *Global Pesticide Campaigner*, vol. 14, Aug. 2004; www.panna.org).

Organic agriculture is not going to disappear. I've never met a farmer who made the switch from conventional to organic and regretted it. Organic farmers make more money. They are no longer handling dangerous chemicals. Their livestock are happier. Their yields are now nearly on par with those of conventional farms, and they are leaving their soil healthier for future generations. By contrast, I know plenty of conventional farmers who are miserable and scared.

A more enlightened federal government would help support farmers who wish to break their chemical addictions. Short of that, the collective power of our spending choices as consumers remains a powerful tool for change. Sales of organic food have increased one hundred fold since 1980 and are predicted to hit $20 billion by 2005. With an average annual growth rate of 20 percent for the past decade, organic food production is now the fastest growing sector of U.S. agriculture. Says a recent issue of *American Banker* magazine in a clear message to lending institutions, "Organic farming is establishing itself as the bright spot in an otherwise bleak picture of U.S. agriculture." Even as organic food has become the darling of chefs, organic cotton has now caught the interest of high-end designers.

Redirecting our food and clothing dollars toward organic farmers is a political decision as well as a lifestyle choice. Organic farms tend to be smaller and therefore keep rural areas populated. They do not contaminate public drinking water supplies, kill off birds and honeybees, and poison farm workers. They require more labor and therefore create jobs. Buying food that is locally grown as well as organic saves fossil fuels and slows urban sprawl caused by the development of failed farms.

Architecture may be the next organic agriculture. The USDA's organic certification program sets standards for the chemical-free growing practices of organic growers. The U.S. Green Building Council is attempting to do something analogous for building design and is promulgating its own standards. The citizen group acting as watchdog for this process is the Healthy Building Network.

No one likes to feel overwhelmed. Or patronized. When trying to coax people toward environmental activism, I seldom emphasize the dire nature of our situation. It is dire, of course. More dire than when Rachel

Carson warned us about its direness. The problem with striking this note, however, is that most folks cannot imagine a response that they could make that would be sufficient to solve the problem. When faced with the prospect of catastrophic ecological ruin, people tend to make one of four choices. They become fatalistic about the situation—imagining that nothing that ANYONE could do at this point would make a difference. (We're doomed.) They avoid thinking about the topic altogether. (Too depressing.) They become survivalists. (I'll buy bottled water.) Or they discount the messenger. (Environmental wacko.)

Recognizing this tricky psychology, some advocates have taken the tack of focusing on the small and the easily do-able. As if dutifully carrying our recyclables out to the curb each week had the power to keep the icecaps frozen and the jet stream from collapsing. Most people know it won't.

Between the overwhelming and the trivial lies another path. It involves encouraging people to seize on a piece of the problem about which they already have a passionate knowledge and to work as hard as they can on that piece. People who love fishing should work on renewable energy: the burning of coal is the number one contributor of mercury into our atmosphere, and mercury contamination has now made the fish of most freshwater rivers and lakes in the United States too poisoned for children to eat. People who golf should challenge their country clubs to embrace organic turf management. Golf courses typically use more pesticides, acre for acre, than farms. Skiers and surfers should tackle global warming. Teachers need to go after air pollution, which contributes to childhood asthma, a leading cause of absenteeism in schools. Lovers of clothing need to compel their dry-cleaning shops to switch over to nontoxic wet-cleaning technology: the chlorinated solvent perchloroethylene that is typically used to dry clean clothes is a leading contaminant of groundwater. It is also a suspected carcinogen.

What I often say to my audiences is that it is now time to play the Save the World Symphony. It is a vast orchestral piece, and you are but one musician. You are not required to play a solo, but you are required to figure out what your instrument is and play it as well as you can.

Because in the end—the environment is not just something else to

worry about. It is connected to all the things we already worry about—
our children, our health, our homeland—and love with all our hearts.

---

[1] Rachel Carson's letter is reprinted in *Lost Woods*, ed. L. Lear, Beacon Press, 1998.

ECONOMICS

WINNING BLUE COLLARS IN RED STATES
JOHN R. MACARTHUR

The Democratic nominee for president has got to blow the whistle on the "free trade" racket—that is, if the party ever wants to retake the White House.

John R. MacArthur is publisher of *Harper's Magazine* and the author of *The Selling of "Free Trade": NAFTA, Washington, and the Subversion of American Democracy.*

Shortly after the election, I happened across a newspaper story—buried amidst the prevailing chatter about how "values" had carried the day for George Bush—suggesting that John Kerry had failed in the waning days of his campaign to "get his economic message across." I laughed, not without bitterness, because the upper class Democrat from Massachusetts essentially had no economic message—at least not one that made any sense to the great mass of red state residents who wear blue collars. Welded by training and inclination to the discredited theories of "free trade"—old-fashioned dogmas that continue to throw large numbers of modern-day employees out of work—Kerry could not overcome the elitist image of an uncaring, out-of-touch windsurfer, a patrician who could parse the writings of David Ricardo and Adam Smith, but wouldn't know a hammer from a nail (or, for that matter, a hammer from a sickle).

The Democratic Party on November 3 found itself in a position similar to Kerry's—out of touch and at sea. Throughout the tiresome post-mortems in the media, almost nobody mentioned that the "people's" party's new minority status was directly traceable to President Bill Clinton's decision to ram the North American Free Trade Agreement down the throat of his own liberal wing as well as that of a diehard Democratic constituency, the formerly powerful institution known as organized labor. Since the passage of NAFTA in the fall of 1993 (and in 2000, of its deadlier cousin Permanent Normal Trading Relations with China), U.S. factory employment had gone into free fall, at least 350,000 manufacturing jobs lost to NAFTA alone. Meanwhile, increases in average hourly wages—for a time still coasting upward on the tech bubble of the 1990's—had ground to a halt at about $8.26 (still well below the 1973 figure of $8.98). Everybody knew that life was getting harder for the working class, that Dad and Mom and Grandpa and Grandma (and Sis and Junior) needed to work more hours or more jobs to make ends meet. But nobody with a sizable audience of voters, outside of Lou Dobbs on CNN, felt obliged to offer any relief beyond slogans (free trade is "win, win") or the magical realism of free trade doctrine ("comparative advantage," "globalization," "creative destruction," etc.).

At the same time, private sector unions, backbone of the former Democratic majority coalition, were losing members to "free trade" at a rate that presaged extinction. By November, 2004, unionized employees made up just eight percent of the total private work force in the U.S., strikes were rare and successful organizing efforts had almost ceased to be. With so many factories shutting down and moving to Mexico and China, there was hardly anybody left to organize besides janitors and retail clerks. Even the Teamsters Union, allegedly America's toughest, had thrown in the towel on NAFTA. In July, while Kerry was "reporting for duty" at the FleetCenter in Boston, Mexican truck drivers, working for a fraction of the wages paid to American drivers, had finally begun transporting Mexican assembled "exports" across the U.S. border and deep into the American heartland. (Of course, the benefits of NAFTA to Mexico were as phony as the ones promised to America: these "made-in-Mexico" "exports" were really just finished products assembled from parts made almost entirely in the U.S. and Canada. Mexican-made components comprised less than one percent of total production at the so-called *maquiladoras*—the assembly points thrown up along the Mexican side of the border—with almost all destined for U.S. consumption.) Homeland security evidently had nothing to do with the economic security of American citizens.

Among the political and media classes, it hardly mattered anymore that "free trade" American style had almost nothing to do with the actual philosophy of its founding theorists. NAFTA and PNTR were always intended as investment agreements designed to protect U.S. capital against expropriation by thieving and corrupt foreign governments. No right-thinking businessman doubted the advantages of cheap labor south of the border ($1 an hour), or of the work ethic in "communist" China, where wage slaves worked for significantly less than they did in Juárez or Nogáles. They just wanted to reduce the risk of their cheap labor profits and physical assets being stolen by radical politicians, as occurred with Mexican oil in 1938, and on a grander scale in Maoist China in 1949. The point of "free trade" treaties was to buy stability for foreign businessmen—to lock in low wages and profits in political environments hostile to genuine, independent labor unions. Under NAFTA, the elimination of what were already very low tariffs was always secondary to the more important goal of tying the hands of untrustworthy natives. Now, if the Mexican government turned nasty and expropriated, the matter would be settled correctly by a U.S. court—and the settlement would be paid in a currency issued by the respectable members of the G-7 club of industrial nations. Pesos are fine—as long as they're for Mexicans.

So, with all those decent-paying factory jobs going abroad, why didn't Kerry exploit the unhappiness of its victims? Why didn't he break with the free trade orthodoxy of Wal-Mart and Wall Street? After all, he had plenty of successful political role models—James Madison, Abraham Lincoln and... Ross Perot. Yes, Ross Perot, who never promised to save anybody's soul, but did promise to try to save their jobs. In his independent run for the presidency in 1992, the eccentric entrepreneur from Texarkana grabbed 19 percent of the popular vote—nearly 20 million voters in all—on an anti-free trade platform. Most of his support came from what we now call "red state" types, an eclectic mixture of reform-minded, conservative Republicans and Reagan Democrats. Perot was so successful sinking George Bush Sr. (Father of NAFTA) that he nearly managed to kill NAFTA itself the following year—this in spite of the enormously sophisticated and well-funded efforts of the Clinton Administration, the Business Roundtable and Newt Gingrich. Perot's anti-NAFTA paperback, *Save Your Job, Save Our Country*, became a best-seller and, different from Kerry, few seemed to begrudge the "billionaire populist" his great wealth.

But NAFTA passed and Clinton reaped both the credit and the blame. In 1994, Gingrich astutely surmised the unhappiness of the Perot supporters (he happily let Clinton and Al Gore associate themselves with NAFTA) and his radical Republicans swept to victory in the House, where they hold the majority still. Many Democrats and unionists were so upset over NAFTA that they didn't bother to vote.

Kerry didn't get the hint. While the big business, anti-union toady Bush (Son of the Father of NAFTA) cynically slapped temporary tariffs on imported steel—a tactic that pleased active and retired steelworkers in traditionally Democratic West Virginia and swing state Pennsylvania— Kerry dithered, proposing weak measures to stem the tide of de-industrialization. As the lion of the anti-free trade movement, Senator Ernest "Fritz" Hollings, put it: "Kerry [was] in the hands of the Philistines and the pollsters," too fearful of his political masters to buck the potent combination of what Hollings calls "ideology backed by money." Clinton had used NAFTA to prove he was a business friendly "New Democrat," and business repaid him handsomely with large PAC contributions that brought the Democrats close to parity in corporate fundraising with the Republicans. It was great for the party managers, but lousy as a vote-getting tactic.

And if Kerry had broken with the free-traders? Wal-Mart/Wall Street would have been furious and some of that anybody-but-Bush money would have dried up. Anti-union Wal-Mart likes cheap imports it can mark up high; Wall Street likes profits guaranteed by the labor racketeers in Mexico and China; both like illegal immigrant labor on the American side of the border—it picks fruits and vegetables for dirt cheap, it cooks and cleans for very little and it busts unions while it undercuts U.S. citizens struggling to make something above the minimum wage. (The *Financial Times* of November 24, 2004 published a story with the headline, "Wal-Mart China Open to Unions," a notion replete with brutal irony since "unions" in China are wholly owned subsidiaries of the government, used, as the FT explains, to "control workers.") That's the money part of the Hollings equation.

Then there's the ideology part. The editorial pages of every major newspaper would have rained down like hell's fury on Kerry, or any Democratic candidate who spoke against the gospel of David Ricardo. "Vile protectionist," pundits would have screamed, from Thomas Friedman to Fred Hiatt to Michael Kinsley. For the true believers, enthusiasm for free trade doctrine borders on religious devotion and high tariffs are the work of the devil himself.

So why rock the boat? Except for his brief flirtation with nonconformity after Vietnam, the go along to get along Kerry never defied the orthodox thinking about any issue—he voted for NAFTA and PNTR as automatically as he voted for the Iraq war resolution. And yet, the Democratic nominee for president has got to blow the whistle on the "free trade" racket—that is, if the party ever wants to retake the White House. As Hollings says, "Have you ever had a pollster that ever served in public office?" Values or no values, there are votes available for a national Democrat who dares to put the economic security of ordinary Americans ahead of the greed and blindness of the free trade lobby.

In 1960, the combined employment of the U.S. textile and apparel industries was close to 2.2 million; as of today it is less than a third of that. "You think we developed a middle class on a cheap shirt?" asks the old Democrat Hollings. "Give me a break. I can tell you right now, the labor unions and the G.I. Bill built the middle class in America." Not to mention high, protective tariffs.

Tell it to a New Democrat.

STOP YAWNING OVER TAXES
MAUD NEWTON

Tax and fiscal policy determine one of the most basic things about our society: what we prioritize enough to pay for, and where the money will come from.

Maud Newton used to practice tax law in Florida under a different name. Now she works as an editor and writer in New York City. She also runs the literary website MaudNewton.com.

The first time I thumbed through the U.S. tax code, I panicked. Against my better judgment, I'd succumbed to my father's wishes and enrolled in law school, and now I was sitting in a basic federal income tax class for law students. Around me sat accounting and finance types who, like my father before them, wanted to learn to help rich people avoid taxes so that they, in turn, would become rich enough to need tax advice.

With a background in British and American literature, I knew I was hopelessly out of my depth. And when the professor asked who'd taken accounting or finance in undergrad, I learned I was one of only two people who hadn't. "It's not too late to drop the class," the professor said.

There at my desk, looking at the Internal Revenue Code, I considered it. The provisions were numbered and divided into subparagraphs and sub-subparagraphs. They had boring, technical names: Section 61 defined "gross income," Section 1031 was devoted to "like-kind exchanges," Section 1250 dealt with "gain on the disposition of real property." I hadn't the foggiest idea what any of this meant, but when the finance type to my right smirked at me and adjusted his starched collar, stubbornness prevailed. I decided to stick it out.

The other accounting-deficient student fled the room. The professor raised an eyebrow, looked at me, and waited. I stayed put. He shook his head and moved on to the problem of "Mr. and Mrs. John Q. Taxpayer" and their $250,000 in adjusted gross income.

By the end of the semester, the language and structure of the Internal Revenue Code had so infiltrated my brain that when my clock radio went off on the morning of my tax final, I dreamed I didn't know how to turn it off. In the dream, I rifled through a drawer and found the clock's operating instructions. They were subdivided into sections and numbered and lettered paragraphs that described the clock and its features in great detail but somehow failed to explain how to turn it off. I woke up late and nearly missed my exam.

Four tax classes later, I graduated from law school. After a brief stint with a litigation firm, I took a job as a tax attorney with Florida's equivalent of the IRS. There I met with corporate tax attorneys who tried to intimidate me with their knowledge and positions. They expected the agency (and me, as its representative) to agree to drastic reductions in legitimate tax assessments against their clients in exchange for their promise to pay a fraction of what was owed. The more often I encountered this attitude, the more tenacious I became.

I developed a reputation as a bit of a hard-ass. Rumor has it that "Don't get Newton, whatever you do," became a familiar refrain in Florida's state tax community. I was 26, heady with power and on a crusade to make corporations own up to their tax liabilities. Since then I've abandoned the practice of law altogether, but I've carried forward the conviction that tax and fiscal policy determine one of the most basic things about our society: what we prioritize enough to pay for, and where the money will come from.

Liberals as a group fail to understand the most basic facets of tax policy. Taxes are complicated, after all, and we have some vague sense that we might have to do some math in order to understand them. So our efforts to oppose conservatives' fiscal shenanigans are almost always doomed. We know Reagan's "trickle-down economics"—the idea that the lower and middle classes benefit from tax cuts handed to the wealthy—just don't make good horse sense, but most of us don't know how to launch rational arguments against them. What's more, we lack the Republican spinmeisters' ability to play fast and loose with economic concepts. So we stand by, hogtied, as they pitch regressive tax policies in such snappy language that the people the policies hurt most eat them up.

Republicans, meanwhile, understand that taxes bore people. They know Democrats will never get the public riled up about "tax cuts that benefit only the wealthiest 2% of Americans," particularly not when the same tax plan sent most members of the middle-class a $300 "tax rebate" check.

In fact, many low-income people applaud the repeal of the "death tax" (the Republicans' nickname for the estate tax). They like the sound of the "simple flat tax" in place of the complex income tax system we have now. Take my mom and stepdad. They have to climb out the window of their late 80's Dodge Aries when the doors stick on rainy days because they can't afford to pay a mechanic, and a few years ago my stepdad had all his teeth extracted because fillings and other routine dental procedures were too expensive. And they think Bush's tax cuts are great. Never mind that they'd never in a million years have seen estate tax liability—in 2002 and 2003, taxpayers had to have more than $1 million in assets before the tax kicked in—and that a revenue-neutral flat tax would mean a massive tax increase for people in their income bracket.

Thanks to the Bush administration, the deficit has skyrocketed, public services are becoming increasingly scarce, and states and localities have increased sales, cigarette, and property taxes. According to figures put out by the U.S. Census, poverty has risen every year since Bush's tax cuts took effect. The number of Americans without health insurance is rising. *New York Times* columnist Paul Krugman has observed that a "crusade against taxes" has dominated American politics for the past 25 years. As a result, he says:

> ...there is now a fundamental mismatch between the benefits Americans expect to receive from the government and the revenues government collect. This mismatch is already having profound effects at the state and local levels: teachers and policemen are being laid off and children are being denied health insurance. The federal government can mask its problems for a while, by running huge budget deficits, but it, too, will eventually have to decide whether to cut services or raise taxes. And we are not talking about minor policy adjustments. If taxes stay as low as they are now, government as we know it cannot be maintained.... Social Security will have to become far less generous; Medicare will no longer be able to guarantee comprehensive medical care to older Americans; Medicaid will no longer provide basic medical care to the poor.[1]

Slowly, beginning with specious Reaganomics, and continuing through Bush's so-called Economic Growth and Tax Relief Reconciliation Act of 2001 and beyond, Republicans have undermined the progressivity of our tax structure, helping the rich get richer and the poor get poorer. Many members of the middle class have begun the long slide toward poverty.

Bush clearly plans to implement more of the same. Less than 24 hours after the presidential election results were in, he characterized his win as a re-election mandate and pledged to continue to pursue his tax agenda.

We've seen the devastating impact of unwise tax polices before.

To briefly get into numerical specifics: A look back to the years before the Great Depression reveals that the highest personal income tax rate was decreased from 58% to 25% in the mid-1920's, and further cut to 24% in 1929, the year of the infamous stock market collapse. The economy foundered until FDR took office. He increased the top rate to 63% and implemented the New Deal, which, in conjunction with World War II, kicked the country into its greatest period of middle-class prosperity.

From the start of World War II until Reagan became President, the upper personal income tax tier *was never less than 70%, and was at times above 90%.* Reagan reduced the top bracket to 50%—probably a fair reduction—and then, despite the country's economic founderings, reduced it again to 28% during his last year in the White House. Bush Senior raised the top rate a bit, to 31%, but the economy was in shambles by the time Clinton took office. He increased the top rate to 39.6%. Within a few years the economy was again on the upswing. (For verification of all rates, see "Statistics of Income Bulletin, Table A: U.S. Individual Income Tax: Personal Exemptions and Lowest and Highest Bracket Tax Rates, and Tax Base for Regular Tax, Tax Years 1913-2003" at the IRS website)   Republicans claim the recovery resulted from Reagan's tax cuts and blame our current economic troubles on Clinton. History suggests the converse.

With his 2001 tax cut, Bush reduced the top marginal personal income tax rate from 39.6% to 35% (the reduction is taking effect gradually, from 2001 to 2006). Between the reduction in income taxes for the wealthy, the estate tax repeal, and the outsourcing of jobs to foreign countries (encouraged by corporate tax loopholes), we're already seeing disastrous results.

Yet the Republicans' catchy and misleading rhetoric—"abolish the death tax," "simplify with a flat tax"—has prevented the public from protesting, or even understanding, the changes. They've also succeeded in painting the Republican Party as the one devoted to practical, fair economics, and the Democratic Party as a group of yahoos who have to be held back from heaping dollars into the waiting arms of lazy, chuckling welfare mothers. They don't acknowledge that Clinton brought the deficit under control, that under Bush it's ballooned to staggering proportions, or that the ballooning is due in large part to the extra money now lining the pockets of the rich and filling the coffers of multinational corporations.

So while liberals tend to focus on overtly humanitarian issues—health care for children, resources for the homeless—we also need to brave the tedium of tax and fiscal policy and oppose tax changes that benefit the wealthy and hurt everyone else. Taxes in a capitalist society are the most important check on the aggregation of wealth in the hands of the 2% of the population that already holds most of it. A progressive tax structure ensures a baseline standard of living for even the poorest Americans. It guarantees funding for education, health care, and social programs that are important to us. If we fail to assert ourselves in tax and fiscal policy debates, we cede the way for Republicans to decide perhaps the most fundamental question on the table: what we as a nation are going to throw our money behind, and whether the money will come from the people and corporations that can afford to pay it.

We need to fight Republicans' false but mesmerizing tax rhetoric with catchy slogans and concepts—but true ones—of our own. And we need to repeat them, as Republicans have repeated theirs for the past 25 years, until people start to listen. Kerry made some strides in this direction, pointing out that Bush's increased deficit result in a $20,000 debt for each child born in the U.S. today—"a 'birth tax,'" Kerry called it, that the child "had no part in creating."[2] For every rant about the "death tax," we should decry the birth tax. Every flat tax rhapsody should be countered with references to corporate welfare and cuts for the rich.

If we stop yawning over tax policy and start shouting instead, maybe people will listen.

---

[1] "The Tax Cut Con," *The New York Times,* September 14, 2003.

[2] "Kerry Slams Bush Over Deficit," CNN.com, April 8, 2004:
http://www.cnn.com/2004/ALLPOLITICS/04/07/election.main/

INTERNATIONAL
RELATIONS

TWO PICTURES OF INTERNATIONAL RELATIONS
MARTHA NUSSBAUM

Patriotism is modeled on the mentality of the sports fan, not on the idea that each nation inhabits a world of human souls, in which all nations ought to strive to preserve human rights and human dignity.

Martha C. Nussbaum is Ernst Freund Distinguished Service Professor at the University of Chicago, with appointments in Philosophy, Law, and Divinity. Her most recent book is *Hiding From Humanity: Disgust, Shame and the Law*, and *Frontiers of Justice: Disability, Nationality, Species Membership* will appear in 2005.

The appalling torture at the Abu Ghraib prison made us ask, "What would lead Americans to act that way?" Now, in the wake of the election, we must continue to press this question. We cannot console ourselves with the thought that the torturers were "other", psychotic sadists, perhaps, or inhabitants of a perverse dehumanizing culture. After all, they were and are us, America's sons and daughters. So, if we can bear to think further, in our grief and shame, we cannot avoid asking the next question: "Is there something in America's political culture that helps explain why these people would act this way?" Indeed, I believe, there is. Because that something is likely to be with us for a long time now, we had better identify it and give it the criticism it deserves.

When people torture and humiliate, they are treating their victims as mere means, objects that they can use at will to satisfy their own desires. They are denying that their victims have a fully human status, a dignity that demands respect, a soul. One sign of that denial is the hooding of the prisoners, concealing the face, the bearer of human expression, the window of the soul. Why should good American soldiers, most of them from backgrounds that gave them a decent ethical or religious education, think like that about their Iraqi prisoners? I think at least one part of the explanation can be found in a shift in America's stance toward the rest of the world.

Throughout the history of international relations, two different conceptions of the relationship between nations have contended against one another. One view holds that the space between nations is a place of naked power and force. The interests that govern foreign relations are those of national security and strength alone. All reference to moral norms is mere hypocrisy or illusion. This view, found already in Thucydides' History of the Peloponnesian War, appears repeatedly, especially when thinkers are trying to show how realistic and unsentimental they are. It was the opponent against which the great seventeenth-century political theorist Hugo Grotius argued for his moral view of international relations. Slightly later, it was Thomas Hobbes's enormously influential view of the situation between nations as a "state of nature," an idea that many subsequent thinkers took over and developed. And today, it is the underpinning of modern "realist" views of foreign relations. The Hobbesian view begins as simple description:

nations are only really motivated by power and security interests. But then a normative note creeps in: this is the grown-up way to see the world, this is the hard-headed way to run the affairs of a nation.

According to the Hobbesian view, then, nations are like sports teams: they aim, and rightly aim, at victory and domination, often including the humiliation of the other side. And although there may be some rules limiting their conduct, they would be right to get 'round those rules whenever national security dictates that they do so. Five hallmarks of the Hobbesian view can be identified; all are prominent in the Bush administration.

First, Hobbesians are likely to believe (with some of President Bush's highest officials) that treaties such as the Geneva Convention need not be observed when it is in the sovereign's interest to diverge from them. Hobbesians are also likely, second, to be sympathetic to the idea of preventive or preemptive war: it is much easy to get the better of an enemy when you get in ahead of their assault on you. They are likely, third, to be skeptical of rules that dictate humane treatment of the enemy: for the other side figures in the view as just that, the *other* side, a looming threat to one's own projects. Noticing and responding to the humanity of the people on the other side is seen as mushy soft-heartedness, even appeasement. The people on the other side are objects that have to be corralled or displaced on the way to an effective pursuit of national security. Fourth, they are likely to have little respect for ideas of territorial integrity or national sovereignty; these moral notions are often checks on the pursuit of self-interest. Finally, their final end is security, and not justice, or lasting peace.

The Hobbesian view keeps on being countered, however, by another very different view of foreign relations. This view was sketched by the Roman politician and philosopher Cicero in the first century B. C.. It provided Hugo Grotius with the basis for his classic work *On the Law of War and Peace* in 1625. Kant developed it influentially in *Perpetual Peace* (1795), imagining it as the basis for a lasting peace among nations. And it is the theoretical basis, today, for the international culture of human rights. This view holds that in the space between nations, even though there is no sovereign and hence no or little positive law, there are still binding moral norms. At the heart of these norms lies the idea of human dignity—of the human being as a creature with a soul, a creature who deserves to be treated as an end, not merely as a means. If something is a mere means, then you can do anything you like to it, so long as it suits your purposes. If someone is an end, that status requires respect: and respect for human dignity rightly constrains all actions of all people, everywhere in the world.

Grotius' first and most fundamental principle was that treaties must be kept: to show respect to human beings requires respecting agreements, even when it is not in one's interest to do so. Second, he connected the idea of respect for humanity with a total ban on preventive or preemptive war: for, although responding to an actual outrage could sometimes be just, he held that responding to a merely possible or imaginary outrage was a way of using other people as mere means to your own ends. He also used the idea of human dignity to frame Western philosophy's first extensive account of the limits on the treatment of people in war, giving particular emphasis to the importance of avoiding dehumanizing or cruel punishments. Fourth, he appealed to human dignity to argue that no human being or nation should be stripped of rights in wartime more than is strictly necessary to prevent aggression to others: thus, property should not be appropriated from the vanquished, members of the enemy population should retain their civil and legal rights. Finally, the end of war should always be a just and lasting peace, and one that preserves human dignity. This also meant that meeting people's economic needs should be part of foreign policy: people should not be made to live in desperate conditions, and "international society" should cooperate to the end of relieving need wherever it occurs.

At one time in the late twentieth century, it looked as if the Grotian view was winning out all around the world. A burgeoning international culture of human rights was garnering increasing acceptance from the community of nations. By now it has generated many valuable international agreements that seek to protect human dignity. The U.S. never fully went along, refusing to ratify many of the most important international human rights documents (including the Convention on the Elimination of All Forms of Discrimination Against Women and the Convention on the Rights of the Child). Nonetheless, there were at least some signs that the U. S. was moving in a Grotian direction, accepting moral constraints on the pursuit of national self-interest and showing respect for the community of nations as a cooperative gathering of dignified human beings who pursue common goals.

The foreign policy of the current administration has jolted us sharply to the Hobbesian side. Nothing is clearer than the contempt of our administration for liberal internationalism and the politics of deliberation and mutual respect. Power, security, getting them before they can get you, these are the way the big boys think. Patriotism is modeled on the mentality of the sports fan, not on the idea that each nation inhabits a world of human souls, in which all nations ought to strive to preserve human rights and human dignity. So many policies express contempt for that moral vision: the treatment of the detainees at Guantanamo; the insistence that anyone deemed an enemy combatant has no right to legal counsel; the doctrine of preventive war itself. Memos have now come to light that express the Hobbesian view that the President can do whatever he likes. He may even disregard the Geneva Convention and other international agreements. We signed them with our fingers crossed, so to speak.

As for the interest in promoting peace in the rest of the world: that has gone by the boards. Aid to educational infrastructure, the Middle East peace talks—all this was ignored, with a combination of arrogance and ignorance that led to a focus on only short-term challenges to our interests. Contempt for long-term allies is only one part of this ugly picture.

The administration's policies are not only unethical, they also run deeply counter to America's true interests. Had we kept the Middle East peace talks going, the U.S. would now be in a good position to influence the Palestinian Authority in a positive direction, knowing all the major players and having some credibility with them. As things are, the idea that we must trust to arch-Hobbesian Condoleezza Rice (who, while

Provost at Stanford, proved an implacable enemy of the Ethics program and showed considerable hostility to the whole project of normative ethical inquiry in philosophy and political theory) to start forging cooperative relations with people in whom our President until very recently took basically no interest, is a scary thought indeed. Think too of education: had we funded schools in Pakistan, rather than attending only to its nuclear capacities, thousands of young men would not have had to attend fundamentalist *madrasas*, where extremism is nourished. Short-sighted policies like these have strengthened the hand of terrorists and extremists.

When the Hobbesian view prevails in high places, should we really be surprised when torture follows? The role of prison guard can easily be abused, in the absence of a robust culture of human rights. When our leaders hold that culture in contempt and suggest the idea of the sports fan as a superior image of hard-headed foreign policy, what should one expect loyal and patriotic soldiers to do? Abu Ghraib, albeit extreme, is no aberration. It is the logical fruit of America's current foreign policy. By their fruits you shall know them.

All of us need to do whatever we can do, placed wherever we are placed, to restore the United States to a fruitful and cooperative membership in "international society." That goal is urgent, if we want a world of peace and justice, where all people will be able to lead decent lives, lives in accordance with human dignity. We have lost an election, but the Grotian vision has not been defeated. We can work for its victory—by writing, by teaching students if we have them, by public speaking and other forms of political action, by giving our money to causes we care about, by work with nongovernmental organizations here and abroad, by talking to our children (if we have them) and to any young people we know about the future of the world, and building in them the spirit of critical openness and compassionate commitment. We do not have the luxury of giving way to self-pity, cynicism, or despair. We must get to work, and so we must have hope—even if only because we need that hope to sustain us in our work. There is still time to change the course of events and to build a future of justice and peace.

However, as we say at the end of Yom Kippur, the gates are closing. The time for change is not indefinitely long. The next few years are crucial for America's future in the world, and for the future of a world in which America's role, well or badly played, is certain to be a large one.

DISSENT

PEACE IN A TIME OF PERPETUAL WAR
MEDEA BENJAMIN

We who oppose the war, and who now represent the majority of Americans, must force our representatives to represent us.

Medea Benjamin is cofounder of the human rights group Global Exchange and the women's peace initiative called Code Pink. She has led numerous delegations to both Iraq and Afghanistan, including delegations of military parents who lost their children in Iraq, and started the International Occupation Watch Center.

Immediately after George Bush declared victory on November 2, 2004, his administration gave the green light for an all-out attack on the Iraqi rebel town of Fallujah. The town was virtually leveled, hundreds of civilians were killed, and over 150,000 became desperate refugees suffering from hunger, cold and disease. And all this after Bush supposedly won the election because of his strong moral values!

During the first debate between Bush and John Kerry, Bush made a pointed comment about moral values. "What distinguishes us from the terrorists," he said somberly, "is that we believe that every life is precious." But according to a report in the prestigious medical journal *The Lancet*, the U.S. occupation of Iraq has cost the lives of over 100,000 civilians.

While the Bush administration rarely acknowledges the death toll among U.S. soldiers, it flatly refuses to talk about Iraqi casualties. When asked about Iraqi deaths, then U.S. Central Command chief General Tommy Franks responded tersely, "We don't do body counts."

The Iraqi government also suppresses casualty figures. Dr. Nagham Mohsen, an official at the Iraqi Health Ministry, was ordered in December 2003 to stop compiling data from hospital records, and journalists were prohibited from entering the morgues.

The first scientific study of the human cost of the Iraq war was done by U.S. and Iraqi researchers, led by School of Public Health in Baltimore. The team surveyed 1,000 households in 33 randomly chosen areas in Iraq. They found that the risk of violent death was 58 times higher in the period since the invasion, and that most of the victims were women and children. While their final horrifying calculation of over 100,000 civilian deaths made front-page news in many parts of the world, the U.S. press barely mentioned it.

A United Nations report released in November 2004 found that severe malnutrition in Iraqi children had almost doubled since the U.S. invasion. This translates to roughly 400,000 Iraqi children suffering from "wasting," a condition characterized by chronic diarrhea and dangerous deficiencies of protein. Iraq's child malnutrition rate now roughly equals that of Burundi, a central African nation torn by more than a decade of war. It is far higher than child malnutrition rates in Uganda and Haiti. And this in a country where, just a generation ago, the biggest nutritional problem for young Iraqis was obesity!

While Iraqis have certainly suffered the most from this war, the cost in lives of U.S. soldiers continues to mount, nearing 1,500 by the end of 2004. Another 10,000 U.S. soldiers were wounded in action, and *thousands* more killed in accidents.

U.S. troops are facing a growing insurgency and the Bush administration has no exit strategy. Even John Kerry, in his run for the presidency, failed to present a convincing exit strategy, partially because he refused to admit that we should never have invaded Iraq to begin with.

There are many good reasons to oppose the occupation of Iraq, from the mounting casualties to the bankrupting of our economy to the increased anti-American feelings it has engendered. But there is one really compelling reason to call for the withdrawal of our troops: the Iraqis want us to leave.

While most Iraqis were delighted with the downfall of Saddam Hussein, they don't want foreign troops occupying their country. A survey of Iraqis sponsored by the U.S. Coalition Provisional Authority in May 2004 showed that most Iraqis say they would feel safer if U.S. forces left immediately. An overwhelming majority, about 80 percent, also said they have "no confidence" in either the U.S. civilian authorities or military forces. If we really believe in democracy, then we should listen to the demands of the majority of Iraqi people and leave their country.

Our demands as a peace movement should be for the U.S. government to make a commitment to withdraw our troops by the end of 2005 at the latest; to pledge that we will not maintain permanent bases in Iraq; and to commit to ending the war profiteering by U.S. companies and give Iraqis the opportunity to rebuild their own country. Once U.S. troops make a commitment to leave, that will open up the possibility of UN or other peacekeepers to come in.

So how do we build a peace movement that can put forward these demands in an effective way? Here are some practical things we can do.

1.Make real the human cost of the war on both U.S. and Iraqi lives.

Since the U.S. invasion in March 2003, the public in most countries throughout the world has seen the horrible pictures of Iraq war victims. The big exception is the U.S. public, which has seen a sanitized version of the war. CNN International regularly shows footage of war victims in its worldwide broadcasts but not on domestic CNN. The world community demands to know the truth, and we should too. Write letters, call and email your local media demanding that they cover the victims of war. If they fail to respond, organize a community delegation to visit them. If they fail to respond to that as well, organize protests at their offices.

Invite an Iraqi-American to come speak to your community about the effects of the occupation. Contact Global Exchange Speakers Bureau for a list of Iraqi and American speakers on the war (www.globalexchange.org).

Regarding the cost of war for U.S. soldiers, ask your local media to read or print a daily casualty toll. Do screenings in your schools and churches of a new video called The Ground Truth that contains poignant interviews with wounded soldiers. To get a copy, go to www.thegroundtruth.org.

If the public were able to see, on a sustained basis, the gory reality of this war—the children without limbs, the wailing mothers, the shivering refugees, the U.S. soldiers coming home in body bags or incapacitated for life—-support would plummet and the war would end.

2. Support military families who are speaking out against the war, and soldiers who are speaking out and refusing to fight.

Military Families Speak Out is a group of over 1,000 families with loved ones in the military. Help get their voices out on the media or invite one of them to speak in your community. Some of them are parents of fallen soldiers, such as Lila Lipscomb of *Fahrenheit 911*, and their testimony is heart-wrenching and compelling.

In the case of Vietnam, dissent within the armed forces itself was critical in ending the war. There is now a new group of soldiers called Iraq

Veterans Against the War that deserves our support. So do the soldiers who are refusing to serve. Over one-third of some 4,000 combat veterans have resisted their call-ups. One of the most public soldiers who refused to return to fight in Iraq is Camilo Mejia, who is serving a one-year prison sentence after being convicted of desertion. "I witnessed the horror of war," said Camilo at his trial, "the firefights, the ambushes, the excessive use of force, the abuse of prisoners. Acting upon my principles became incompatible with my role in the military. By putting my weapon down I chose to reassert myself as a human being."

We also need to support counter-recruitment efforts, efforts that provide young people—particularly in poor communities—with a truthful picture of the risks of joining the military and of their other options for employment and education. See www.objector.org for a list of groups doing counter-recruitment, general support for soldiers (including a GI Rights Hotline), and advice for those who want to apply for conscientious objector status.

3. Pressure Congress to cut off further funding, investigate war profiteering and cut Halliburton from the government dole.

While the Republicans took us into this war and therefore bear the bulk of the blame, the Democrats have been their enablers. All Democratic congress members, with the exception of Congresswoman Barbara Lee (D-CA), voted for using war as a response to 9/11, and the majority of Democrats went along with the October 2002 vote to use force in Iraq. In the meantime, more and more Americans oppose the war.

We who oppose the war, and who now represent the majority of Americans, must force our representatives to represent us. We must demand that they stop spending the obscene amount of $2 billion a week to occupy Iraq and that they oppose any further funding or additional troops.

We must also call on Congress to stop government agencies from giving contracts to U.S. companies for "rebuilding" Iraq. Iraqis have some of the best engineers and builders in the world, and are totally capable of rebuilding their own country. Congress should investigate more fully the charges of war profiteering against U.S. companies, particularly

Halliburton. In fact, there is an on-going FBI probe of Halliburton for war profiteering. We should demand that Congress stop all monies to Halliburton while charges are pending and if found guilty, that the company be banned from receiving any future government contracts.

4. Strengthen local peace work and bring the cost of the war home.

The anti-war coalition must reach out to broader sectors of the community, especially religious groups, labor, communities of color and students. We must make clear the connections between the $200 billion squandered on Iraq and the cuts that communities across the U.S. are facing in health care, education and vital social services. The amazing website www.nationalpriorities.org will give you an estimate of the cost of the war for your city and state.

Get local churches, labor unions, student governments and city councils to pass resolutions against the occupation. Hundreds of such resolutions were passed before the war began; we need to revive that energy in the call to bring the troops home. In November 2004, the city of San Francisco actually had an anti-occupation measure on the ballot, and it passed overwhelmingly. Similar ballot initiatives or resolutions could be passed in cities all over the country.

The local peace coalitions should work closely with the national umbrella group United for Peace and Justice. This is the organization that put together the largest anti-war rallies, including the massive February 15, 2003 rally that took place in New York City and hundreds of cities around the country—and the world.

5. Build the global coalition

February 15, 2003 was indeed an amazingly powerful day when "the world said no to war." We need to strengthen the global anti-war coalition and not just organize joint rally days, but joint campaigns. These could be campaigns against companies profiting from war, or campaigns to get countries that are still part of the "coalition forces" to withdraw (by the end of 2004, at least 15 of the original 32 members of the coalition had either left Iraq or had announced their intention to leave).

Another international campaign could be focused on the United Nations. We should consider pushing the United Nations—both at the Security Council and the General Assembly—to call for a swift timeline for the withdrawal of foreign military forces from Iraq.

6. Support efforts to decrease our dependence on oil.

While the U.S. invasion of Iraq was not SOLELY about oil, it is certainly true that if broccoli were Iraqi's main export, we would not have invaded. It's also true that until we get off our dependence on oil, we will continue to have policies in the Middle East tie us to undemocratic regimes like Saudi Arabia or push us to invade countries like Iraq to control their oil.

There are plenty of ways to start breaking our oil addiction, including a massive investment in solar and wind power (see www.appolloproject.org), promoting fuel efficient vehicles (see www.jumpstartford.org), and focusing on conservation and efficiency (see www.rmi.org).

George Bush took the 2004 election as a mandate to continue this illegal, immoral war in Iraq. It is up to us, the American people, to rebel against Bush's arrogant empire-building. It is up to us, caring, compassionate American people, to force the Bush administration to change course, start respecting international law, and take our rightful place as one among many in the family of nations.

KEEP TAKING IT TO THE STREETS
LESLIE CAGAN

I start from the belief that change—fundamental, systemic change—is secured when massive numbers of people are involved.

For almost 40 years, Leslie Cagan has worked in peace and social justice movements locally and nationally. Her writings appear in numerous anthologies, journals, newspapers and on-line outlets. Cagan is presently the National Coordinator of United for Peace and Justice, the nation's largest antiwar coalition with more than 850 local and national organizations. U.P.J. led, most recently, the August 29, 2004 demonstration of over 500,000 people in New York City on the eve of the Republican National Convention.

I woke up on Nov. 3rd forced to consider what is happening in this country in a new way. It was not so much that everything had changed overnight, but rather that the challenges we face and the context we work in were now smack in front of us in all of their stark and frightening reality. It is not just that these people are still in power, as awful as that is. These people, and the political/ideological foundation they move from, have the support of tens of millions of people in this nation. The fundamentalist right wing has a real base. Yes, people have been lied to and yes the politics of fear has been fine tuned and expertly executed by Karl Rove and company. But it would be short sighted to deny the reality: 40 years of organizing by the ultra-right (since the defeat of Barry Goldwater in 1964) have resulted in their consolidation of power and the control they now have.

My work has often been helping to put people into the streets—organizing public protests of all sizes and shapes for peace and social justice movements. Over the years people have asked, why protest, what's the point of putting all that time and effort and resources into demonstrations when there doesn't usually seem to be any pay off, any immediate or noticeable change created by these actions? Fair question.

I start from the belief that change—fundamental, systemic change—is secured when massive numbers of people are involved. Whatever positive contributions are made by small elites or even vanguard parties, it is the direct involvement of tremendous numbers of people in the activities of social change movements that makes the critical difference. Just think about the history of this country: the battles against slavery or for women's suffrage; the fight for a forty-hour work week or against child labor; the movement to end the Vietnam War; and the ongoing struggles against racism and for civil rights. Nothing moves forward without the direct involvement of masses of people.

We must now move forward in two major areas, simultaneously. We need to keep those people who are already with us fully engaged and mobilized—which includes calling on them to keep coming out to the full range of public protest activities. At the same time, we need to strengthen our commitment to organizing. We need to understand that the companion to our mobilizing must be organizing. There are people in every corner of this country, in blue and red states alike, waiting for us to knock on their doors and share our ideas. We need to bring our message to the people whose neighborhoods and schools and religious centers and workplaces we share.

Organizers face a host of challenges, but perhaps none greater than how to keep people involved in our movements. Once the educational work is in place and the inspirational projects have moved people, what are we offering people as vehicles for their direct involvement? There are lots of things people can, and should do, in addition to the marches and rallies: lobby elected officials, organize unions at their workplaces, write letters to the editor and guest columns for their local papers, take nonviolent action that interrupts business as usual, send humanitarian aid to people suffering because of our governments policies, and much more.

Through it all, we need to keep people connected and show the strength we do have. Public action, public protest, is a valuable tool for expressing our collective or community strength, and even to show the potential power of our movements.

If you were with us on the streets of New York City on August 29, 2004, the day before the Republican National Convention opened you know what I'm talking about. 500,000 strong, we marched against the Bush Agenda, and stood up for our very right to protest, which had been under attack by NYC officials.

If you were in Washington, D.C. for the April 2004 march for women's lives with a million other people, or if you were in NYC on Feb. 15, 2003, or in Seattle in December 1999, or part of the 1987 Gay/Lesbian Rights march, or the 1963 civil rights march, or other mass events, then you also know what I mean.

There is nothing quite like the feeling of gathering in large numbers with people from diverse communities, the overwhelming majority of whom you do not know personally, publicly expressing a common point of view, or making a unified demand. In a culture that seeks to homogenize our thoughts and limit our options, creating space for an alternative point of view can be a profound act. There are, after all, so few vehicles for public expression in this culture, so few opportunities to make our voices heard. And that is one of the reasons we gather in public protest: to make our voices heard!

One of the often unmentioned reasons to organize protest demonstrations has to do with the energy created when people gather in common cause. This doesn't only happen when massive numbers assemble, and in fact, some of the most empowering experiences happen in smaller numbers. But whatever the size, the coming together and taking unified action often inspires, motivates and energizes people for the work in between the demonstrations.

We organize protests as a way to send a message to those in power and those seeking power. When we marched past Madison Square Garden on August 29th we were certainly sending a message to George W. Bush and the Republican Party. At the same time, we were sending a message to John Kerry and the Democratic Party. That is, whoever won the presidency, the movement for peace and justice is strong and growing in this country, and we will continue to make our demands and fight for what is right, regardless of who sits in the White House or controls the Congress.

Our public protests are also opportunities to send a message to people in our city or nation, and even around the world. If our message gets through, they are hearing about what we think and what we want. Beyond that we are telling people it is vitally important that they too speak out. Again, if change comes because massive numbers of people are involved in our movements, then we must always be encouraging new people to join us. And by our public actions we begin to model new ways of action, new ways for people to be engaged.

As we think about the work ahead we have to be aware of the need to keep people mobilized and to keep putting people into the streets. Sometimes it will be local actions, or periodically, we will need to gather in large, national events. Not all of our actions will or should take the same form. Bayard Rustin and John Lewis knew that in 1963 it was time to bring people to Washington, D.C., but that did not mean the local marches and sit-ins and vigils in cities around the country stopped or were less meaningful. On June 12, 1982 a million people marched and rallied for nuclear disarmament. As powerful and important as that demonstration was, it did not take away from the importance of 1400 people committing nonviolent civil disobedience at the UN missions of the then-five nuclear states just two days later.

In the context of a government controlled by fundamentalist right-wingers with an agenda that includes the shutting down of dissent and opposition, it is even more vital that our work includes the mobilizing of large numbers of people to participate in public protest activities. Their attempts to stifle dissent is real: $25 million of the supplemental budget for the Iraq war went into policing operations during the protests in Miami at the time of the FTAA meetings in Nov. 2003; millions more from the Iraq budget went to policing during the protests in Georgia at the time of the G8 summit in June 2003; the Secret Service regularly keeps protesters out of sight and sound whenever the president or vice-president makes a public appearance; in NYC United for Peace and Justice was denied a march permit for the massive antiwar protest on Feb. 15, 2003 and then denied a rally permit for Central Park for the historic August 29, 2004 protest. All around the country organizers report on unnecessary shows of police strength, spying on groups and other forms of intimidation.

We should aim to get more people to our vigils and pickets and marches and rallies, whether these are neighborhood demonstrations or major national mobilizations. We also need to develop more creative ways to publicly protest, invent forms of protest that directly challenge power. For instance, many of us in the antiwar movement are exploring ideas for protests that define our resistance to the ongoing war in Iraq and the empire-building, permanent war posture of the Bush administration. In the months ahead I'm sure there will be more nonviolent civil disobedience at military facilities or Congressional offices or even mainstream media outlets where they seem to have such a hard time telling the full story in an honest way.

We need to do all of this and, as I said earlier: our energies and efforts need to also be directed into ongoing organizing campaigns. If we give short shrift to the organizing work then our mobilizing simply will not grow and will not become stronger. By organizing I mean having direct personal contact with people: knocking on doors, tabling at malls and supermarkets, talking to people at the schools and day care centers we take our kids to, discussing issues at gatherings in religious institutions, trade unions and schools. As powerful as the Internet is and as wonderful as it is getting our story into the media, there is nothing like actually talking with people.

Our movements for peace and justice need to find new ways to work together, to forge a deeper unity. There's been a lot of talk about morality and moral issues playing a key role in the 2004 elections. It's past time for us to articulate our morality and our vision of what this nation could be, based on the moral values of peace, social and economic justice, equality and freedom, honoring the sovereignty of other nations, sharing - not plundering - resources, commitment to human and civil rights for every single person, and respect for the environment and the planet we all share.

The good news is that there IS movement in this country. In the days following the November 2nd election our office got calls from people all around the country. People were asking what comes next, but mostly they were communicating something critically important. The thousands of groups working on scores of issues have not closed shop and activists have not given up. Posing the question, what comes next, implies the commitment to keep going. Yes, we need to understand what we are up against and the obstacles we have to overcome. To paraphrase Sweet Honey In the Rock, we who believe in freedom will not rest!

Let's take our message and our vision to the streets, always inviting more and more people to march with us, to stand with us, to demand and make the changes that we know must be made.

APPENDIX

EQUAL TIME #1:
MANIFESTO
GEORGE SAUNDERS

Last Thursday, my organization, People Reluctant To Kill for an Abstraction, orchestrated an overwhelming show of force around the globe.

George Saunders is the author *of CivilWarLand in Bad Decline* and *Pastoralia.*

A press release from PRKA

Last Thursday, my organization, People Reluctant To Kill for an Abstraction, orchestrated an overwhelming show of force around the globe.

At precisely 9 in the morning, working with focus and stealth, our entire membership succeeded in simultaneously beheading no one. At 10, Phase II began, during which our entire membership did not force a single man to suck another man's penis. Also, none of us blew himself/herself up in a crowded public place. No civilians were literally turned inside out via our powerful explosives. In addition, at 11, in Phase III, zero (0) planes were flown into buildings.

During Phase IV, just after lunch, we were able to avoid bulldozing a single home. Furthermore, we set, on roads in every city, in every nation in the world, a total of zero (0) roadside bombs which, not being there, did not subsequently explode, killing/maiming a total of nobody. No bombs were dropped, during the lazy afternoon hours, on crowded civilian neighborhoods, from which, it was observed, no post-bomb momentary silences were then heard. These silences were, in all cases, followed by no unimaginable, grief-stricken bellows of rage, and/or frantic imprecations to a deity. No sleeping baby was awakened from an afternoon nap by the sudden collapse and/or bursting into flame of his/her domicile during Phase IV.

In the late afternoon (Phase V), our membership focused on using zero (0) trained dogs to bite/terrorize naked prisoners. In addition, no stun guns, rubber batons, rubber bullets, tear gas, or bullets were used, by our membership, on any individual, anywhere in the world. No one was forced to don a hood. No teeth were pulled in darkened rooms. No drills were used on human flesh, nor were whips or flames. No one was reduced to hysterical tears via a series of blows to the head or body, by us. Our membership, while casting no racial or ethnic aspersions, skillfully continued not to rape, gang-rape, or sexually assault a single person. On the contrary, during this late-afternoon phase, many of our membership flirted happily and even consoled, in a nonsexual way, individuals to whom they were attracted, putting aside their sexual feelings out of a sudden welling of empathy.

As night fell, our membership harbored no secret feelings of rage or, if they did, meditated, or discussed these feelings with a friend until such time as the feelings abated, or were understood to be symptomatic of some deeper sadness.

It should be noted that, in addition to the above-listed and planned activities completed by our members, a number of unplanned activities were completed by part-time members, or even nonmembers.

In London, a bitter homophobic grandfather whose grocery bag broke open gave a loaf of very nice bread to a balding gay man who stopped to help him. A stooped toothless woman in Tokyo pounded her head with her hands, tired beyond belief of her lifelong feelings of anger and negativity, and silently prayed that her heart would somehow be opened before it was too late. In Syracuse, New York, holding the broken body of his kitten, a man felt a sudden kinship for all small things.

Even declared nonmembers, it would appear, responded to our efforts. In Chitral, Pakistan, for example, a recent al-Qaida recruit remembered the way an elderly American tourist once made an encouraging remark about his English, and how, as she made the remark, she touched his arm, like a mother. In Gaza, an Israeli soldier and a young Palestinian, just before averting their eyes and muttering insults in their respective languages, exchanged a brief look of mutual shame.

Who are we? A word about our membership.

Since the world began, we have gone about our work quietly, resisting the urge to generalize, valuing the individual over the group, the actual over the conceptual, the inherent sweetness of the present moment over the theoretically peaceful future to be obtained via murder. Many of us have trouble sleeping and lie awake at night, worrying about something catastrophic befalling someone we love. We rise in the morning with no plans to convert anyone via beating, humiliation, or invasion. To tell the truth, we are tired. We work. We would just like some peace and quiet. When wrong, we think about it awhile, then apologize. We stand under awnings during urban thunderstorms, moved to thoughtfulness by the troubled, umbrella-tinged faces rushing by. In moments of crisis, we pat one another awkwardly on the back, mumbling shy truisms. Rushing to an appointment, remembering a friend who has passed away, our eyes well with tears and we think: Well, my God, he could be a pain, but still I'm lucky to have known him.

This is PRKA. To those who would oppose us, I would simply say: We are many. We are worldwide. We, in fact, outnumber you. Though you are louder, though you create a momentary ripple on the water of life, we will endure, and prevail. Join us.

Resistance is futile.

EQUAL TIME #2:
WE PAID FOR EIGHT YEARS
MONET OLIVER D'PLACE

One thing is certain: This administration will leave no Billionaire behind.

As the National "Get on the Limo" Tour Coordinator, Monet Oliver d'Place—a.k.a. Marco Ceglie—spent 3 months on the road in his top-hat and tuxedo, reaching voters in 28 cities across 12 swing states. He is now co-Schmoozer in Chief for Billionaires for Bush and author of the upcoming novel *Surveillance*. He wrote this piece with help from the highly valued and never paid staff at Billionaires for Bush Ivan Aston-Martin (Chris Ditto), Meg A. Bucks (Elissa Jiji), Robin Eublind (Paul Bartlett), and Tex Shelter (David McCarthy).

As activists for the rich elite, the very rich elite, and the very very rich elite, Billionaires for Bush couldn't be more delighted with our namesake's presidential victory. Never before has one man done so much for so few at the expense of so many, huzzah!

Dressed in our tuxedoes and top hats, evening gowns and tiaras, Billionaires for Bush, and our pampered blue-blooded progeny, look forward to continuing what has been a continuous four-year party for the privileged.

As Billionaires, we raise our martini glasses and thank the middle class who voted for our economic interest in spite of their own. We would also like to thank the swing states that purchased our paperless voting machines and the front line heroes who valiantly, and shamelessly, blocked the vote. The heroes include such stars as Nathan Sproul, whose GOP-funded Voters Outreach of America has been accused of shredding Democratic voter registration forms in Nevada and Oregon, J. Kenneth Blackwell, Ohio's Secretary of State, who invented and then enforced his own rule that voter applications be printed on 80-pound card stock after voter registration in Democratic counties increased 250%, and Florida's Secretary of State Glenda Hood, who tried to block blacks from voting but not Hispanics, who were more likely to vote Republican. These heroes reinforced our core belief that it's not who votes that counts, it's who counts the votes.

A Democratic victory would have meant a changing of the guard in Washington, and that would have meant disclosing the lobbyists who wrote the 2001 energy policy, revealing the White House staffer who leaked Valerie Plame's covert CIA status to the press, and incarceration for Kenneth Lay, but now our secrets are safe.

For us Billionaires, the election results came as no surprise. We paid for eight years, and while our investment has reaped unprecedented dividends, with lucrative war profiteering, corporate welfare, a massive tax shift, pollution exemptions, no bid contracts, and Camp David sleepovers, we know the best is still to come.

If the next four years are any guide, we can watch excitedly as two more countries are invaded, an additional $2 trillion is added to the deficit, the minimum wage remains frozen at $5.15, the tax burden continues to shift to the middle class, another million jobs are outsourced, and the word "accountability" continues to be preceded by the word "no." And while the president's first term may have benefited from a Republican controlled senate and house, his second term has something new: a mandate. One thing is certain: This administration will leave no Billionaire behind. In fact, we Billionaires are so confident of the return on our investment we proudly lay out our agenda for the next four years.

Environmental Commerce

The environment will be our easiest target; simply put, we will continue to loot the greatest bank on earth: Earth. Resources like oil, natural gas, coal, trees, and clean air are like handbags left behind at a party—ready for the taking. Taking the "protectionism" out of the Environmental Protection Agency (EPA) in the last four years is not enough, though. Following the example of Vladimir Putin, the EPA will be placed under the Department of Commerce. Only then will we be able to recognize old growth forests for the Victoria's Secret catalogues that they have always wanted to become. And the benefit of the Wealthy Forest initiative: you can't have a forest fire without a forest! As for the Alaskan National Wildlife Refuge: drill it dry. After all, what has a caribou done for you lately?

Iraq

Iraq, with its massive reliance on corporate contractors, its no bid contracts, and its poverty draft, has ensured that both fortunate sons and wartime profiteers remain protected. The message to the world is clear: "There is no such thing as foreign oil." And with the most profitable military industrial complex in the world, who needs more allies than Poland, Britain, and Poland?

Reigning in Free Speech

The *Washington Post* and the *New York Times* have wrapped themselves in the first amendment too many times. We are ready to shift to a new media paradigm and Michael Powell is leading the way at the FCC. Powell's new "fee speech" policy puts a price on freedom by fining broadcasters large sums for airing what a panel has determined to be indecent.

Elimina—er, Privatization of Social Security

Moving the money set aside for seniors into individual risk-based retirement accounts is long overdue. It is time to shift the burden of care for the elderly from the nation to, well, the elderly. The elderly poor, that is. The rich have no need for social security. Furthermore, there is no reason those of us in the top 1% should not profit from such a profound shift, and nothing is more eagerly anticipated on Wall Street than the arrival of 100 million new and inexperienced investors. And if another Enron should go under, causing millions of the elderly, infirm and retired to lose their savings? So what? Enron never had to pay back a dime to those who were left in the cold; why should we? We'll sell it by calling it "choice". Everyone loves choice, but we know what it really is: a windfall for savvy Wall Street execs and us, the Billionaires.

Making the Middle Class Tax Burden Permanent

We must continue the drive to lay a heavier tax on wages, while eliminating all taxes on wealth. Though we've made great strides in the last four years reducing taxes on unearned income like dividends, we must exploit our successful campaign that convinced the American public that the tax code is a system that "can't be fixed." Now is the time to institute a flat tax; wherein everyone pays the same percentage, regardless of income or net worth. This ensures that the poor and working class won't skip out on their responsibility to serve the wealthy, in this case by paying more of the tax burden while we pay less across the board. The flat tax would save us a fortune on accountants alone, who now spend the better part of their time figuring out ways to help us avoid paying what we rightfully owe. Sure—everyone else will feel the pinch of higher sales taxes, higher consumption taxes, and higher income taxes, but our tax rate will come down nicely, providing yet another boom to the wealthy. And, if we find the

Treasury can no longer pay for education, public lands, and first responders, our private companies will be ready to step in—for those who can afford to pay, that is.

Ending the Dynasty Tax

We won't rest until we can safely pass our estates down to our oldest legitimate male heir—tax-free. The Dynasty luxury tax unfairly discriminates against not only billionaires, but also those with fortunes over $100 million!

Corporate Welfare

We will continue to reward the Bush campaign's top donors, known as "Pioneers" and "Rangers," with lucrative corporate welfare deals. Governor Pataki has set the mark by liberating the Community Development Block Grants earmarked for whiney 9/11 economic victims, the unemployed and small businesses, while giving out hundreds of millions of dollars and contracts to the loyal rich elite, like Bush Pioneer buddies Roland Betts and Tom Bernstein, who will build Free-the-Rich Hall at Ground Zero.

Defending Dick Cheney

The Vice President has been embroiled in more scandals than anyone can count, including: overseeing Enron-style accounting at Halliburton, the secret energy task force, Supreme Court cronyism, arranging no-bid contracts, dodging the draft repeatedly, bribery of Nigerian officials, and doing business with Iran, Iraq and Libya. The Billionaires will continue to remind America that everything they have ever read about the man is a lie—"Dick Cheney is Innocent!"

So what will the Billionaires be doing under George W. Bush's second term? As long as there are politicians to buy, jobs to outsource, golden parachutes to wear, workers to exploit, countries to invade, foreign oil to tap, and ice sculptures urinating fine Russian vodka… the Billionaires will be there, lobbying for the corporate elite in top hats and tiaras every step of the way.

Though this is an ambitious agenda, the Republican stranglehold, er, majority in Washington will ensure its easy passage. But we must remain vigilant, for our domination is not secure.

Organizations like MoveOn, ACT, Democracy for America, Sierra Club, The Center for American Progress and others will be fighting us every step of the way. These groups are actively engaged in exposing us as the sole beneficiaries of the Republican Agenda. We must keep this movement, this new Progressive Momentum from becoming a Progressive Majority.

Therefore we call upon all people of extraordinary power and privilege to join us. Visit our website (billionairesforbush.com) to find which of our 100 chapters is nearest you. Then dust off that smoking jacket, pull on those evening gloves, warm up that limo, and help us show the world that you can speak power to truth.

HUZZAH!

Websites mentioned throughout the book,
or relevant to particular sections:

STANDING OUR GROUND IN THE FIGHT
FOR JUSTICE AND STRONG DEMOCRACY
JAMIN RASKIN

MoveOn, www.moveon.org

KERRY WON
GREG PALAST
Greg Palast, www.GregPalast.com
TomPaine.com

OUR MANDATE: MAKING MEDIA MATTER
DANNY SCHECHTER

MediaAlliance, media-alliance.org
MediaChannel, www.Mediachannel.org
Weapons of Mass Deception, www.wmdthefilm.com
The News Dissector's weblog,
www.newsdissector.org/weblog/

RECLAIMING THE MEDIA FOR
A PROGRESSIVE FEMINIST FUTURE
JENNIFER L. POZNER

Fairness and Accuracy in Reporting, www.fair.org
Center for International Media Action,
www.mediaactioncenter,org
Democracy Now, www.democracynow.org/
Free Press, www.FreePress.net
Reclaim The Media, www.ReclaimTheMedia.org
Media Alliance, www.Media-Alliance.org
Women In Media & News, www.WIMNonline.org
Independent Media Center, Indymedia.org
Paper Tiger Television, PaperTiger.org

FIGHTING WORDS FOR A SECULAR AMERICA
ROBIN MORGAN

Americans United for Separation of Church and
State,www.au.org
Freedom from Religion Foundation, www.ffrf.org
People for the American Way, www.pfaw.org
Texas Faith Network, www.tfn.org
Feminist.com

REPUBLICANS BANK ON BLACK EVANGELICALS
TO HELP THEM KEEP WINNING
EARL OFARI HUTCHINSON

The Hutchinson Report, www.thehutchinsonreport.com

THE OBLIGATION TO ENDURE... AGAIN...
SANDRA STEINGRABER

Toxics Release Inventory, www.rtknet.org
Scorecard, www.scorecard.org
Stockholm Convention on Persistent Organic Pollutants,
www.pops.int
Canadian Cancer Society, www.cancer.ca
Pesticide Action Network of North America,
www.panna.org/
The Collaborative on Health and the Environment,
www.protectingourhealth.org

STOP YAWNING OVER TAXES
MAUD NEWTON

Internal Revenue Service,
www.irs.gov/pub/irs-soi/03inta.xls

PEACE IN A TIME OF PERPETUAL WAR
MEDEA BENJAMIN

Global Exchange Speakers Bureau,
www.globalexchange.org
The Ground Truth, www.thegroundtruth.org
Military Families Speak Out, www.mfso.org
Iraq Veterans Against the War, www.ivaw.org
Camilo Mejia, www.freecamilo.org
National Priorities, www.nationalpriorities.org
United for Peace and Justice, www.unitedforpeace.org
Apollo Project, Inc., www.apolloproject.org
Jumpstart Ford, www.jumpstartford.org
The Rocky Mountain Institute, www.rmi.org
Code Pink, www.codepinkalert.org
International Occupation Watch Center,
www.occupationwatch.org

KEEP TAKING IT TO THE STREETS
LESLIE CAGAN

United for Peace and Justice, www.unitedforpeace.org
Counter-Inaugural, www.counter-inaugural.org

WE PAID FOR EIGHT YEARS
MONET OLIVER D'PLACE

Billionaires for Bush, www.billionairesforbush.com

ABOUT THE EDITORS

Dennis Loy Johnson and Valerie Merians are the publishers of Melville House. They previously edited the book *Poetry After 9-11*. Merians is a sculptor and writer whose criticism has appeared in newspapers including *The Milwaukee Journal Sentinel* and *Art Week*. Johnson's fiction has won a Pushcart Prize and National Endowment for the Arts award, and his journalism has appeared in publications ranging from *USA Today* and Salon.com to the wires of the Associated Press. He is the author of the book, *The Big Chill: The Great, Unreported Story of the Bush Inauguration Protest.*